Henry Wac

by Thomas V

MW00929492

HENRY WADSWORTH LONGFELLOW

CHAPTER I

LONGFELLOW AS A CLASSIC

The death of Henry Wadsworth Longfellow made the first breach in that well-known group of poets which adorned Boston and its vicinity so long. The first to go was also the most widely famous. Emerson reached greater depths of thought; Whittier touched the problems of the nation's life more deeply; Holmes came personally more before the public; Lowell was more brilliant and varied; but, taking the English-speaking world at large, it was Longfellow whose fame overshadowed all the others; he was also better known and more translated upon the continent of Europe than all the rest put together, and, indeed, than any other contemporary poet of the English-speaking race, at least if bibliographies afford any test. Add to this that his place of residence was so accessible and so historic, his personal demeanor so kindly, his life so open and transparent, that everything really conspired to give him the highest accessible degree of contemporary fame. There was no literary laurel that was not his, and he resolutely declined all other laurels; he had wealth and ease, children and grandchildren, health and a stainless conscience; he had also, in a peculiar degree, the blessings that belong to Shakespeare's estimate of old age,--"honor, love, obedience, troops of friends." Except for two great domestic bereavements, his life would have been one of absolutely unbroken sunshine; in his whole career he never encountered any serious rebuff, while such were his personal modesty and kindliness that no one could long regard him with envy or antagonism. Among all the sons of song there has rarely been such an instance of unbroken and unstained success.

Yet the fact that his death took place twenty years ago may justly raise the question how far this wave of success has followed his memory, or how far the passage of time has impaired his traditional influence; and here we must compare a variety of tests and standards to ascertain the result. Some analysis of this kind may well precede any new attempt to delineate his career.

The editor of one of the great London weeklies said to an American traveller not many years ago, "A stranger can hardly have an idea of how familiar many of our working people, especially women, are with Longfellow. Thousands can repeat some of his poems who have never read a line of Tennyson and probably never heard of Browning." This passage I take from an admirable recent sketch by Professor Edwin A. Grosvenor of Amherst College, one of the most cosmopolitan of Americans, who spent seven years as professor of history at Robert College, Constantinople. He goes on to tell how, in the largest private library in the Ottoman Empire, the grand vizier showed him as his favorite book a large volume of Longfellow, full of manuscript comments in Turkish on the margin, adding that he knew some of the poems by heart. Professor Grosvenor was at one time--in 1879--travelling by steamer from Constantinople to Marseilles with a Russian lady who had been placed under his escort, and whose nationality could have been detected only by her marvellous knowledge of half a dozen languages beside her own. A party of passengers had been talking in French of Victor Hugo, when the Russian lady exclaimed in English to the last speaker, "How can you, an American, give to him the place that is occupied by your own Longfellow? Longfellow is the universal poet. He is better known, too, among foreigners, than any one except their own poets!" She then repeated the verses beginning, "I stood on the bridge at midnight," and added, "I long to visit Boston, that I may stand on the bridge." Then an English captain, returning from the Zulu war, said, "I can give you something better than that," and recited in a voice like a trumpet,--

"Tell me not, in mournful numbers, Life is but an empty dream."

Presently a gray-haired Scotchman began to recite the poem,--

"There is no flock, however watched and tended, But one dead lamb is there!"

An American contributed "My Lost Youth," being followed by a young Greek temporarily living in England, who sang "Stars of the Summer Night." Finally the captain of the steamer, an officer of the French navy detailed for that purpose, whom nobody had suspected of knowing a word of English, recited, in an accent hardly recognizable, the first verse of "Excelsior," and when the Russian lady, unable to understand him, denied the fact of its being English at all, he replied, "Ah, oui, madame, a vient de votre Longfellow" (Yes, madam, that is from your Longfellow). Six nationalities had thus been represented, and the Russian lady said, as they rose from the table, "Do you suppose there is any other poet of any country, living or dead, from whom so many of us could have quoted? Not one. Not even Shakespeare, or Victor Hugo, or Homer."{1}

One has merely to glance at any detailed catalogue of the translations from Longfellow's works--as for instance that given in the appendix to this volume--to measure the vast extent of his fame. The list includes thirty-five versions of whole books or detached poems in German, twelve in Italian, nine each in French and Dutch, seven in Swedish, six in Danish, five in Polish, three in Portuguese, two each in Spanish, Russian, Hungarian, and Bohemian, with single translations in Latin, Hebrew, Chinese, Sanskrit, Marathi, and Judea-German--yielding one hundred versions altogether, extending into eighteen languages, apart from the original English. There is no evidence that any other English-speaking poet of the last century has been so widely appreciated.

Especially is this relative superiority noticeable in that wonderful literary cyclopedia, the vast and many-volumed catalogue of the British Museum. There, under each author's name, is found not merely the record of his works in every successive edition, but every secondary or relative book, be it memoir, criticism, attack, parody, or translation; and it is always curious to consider the relative standing of American and English authors under this severe and inexorable test. The entries or items appearing in the interleaved catalogue under the name of Tennyson, for instance, up to September, 1901, were 487; under Longfellow, 357; then follow, among English-writing poets, Browning (179), Emerson (158), Arnold (140), Holmes (135), Morris (117), Lowell (114), Whittier (104), Poe (103), Swinburne (99), Whitman (64). The nearest approach to a similar test of appreciation in the poet's own country is to be found in the balloting for the new Hall of Fame, established by an unknown donor on the grounds of the New York University with the avowed object of creating an American Westminster Abbey. The names of those who were to appear in it were selected by a board of one hundred judges carefully chosen from men of all occupations and distributed over every State in the Union; and these balloted for the first hundred occupants of the Hall of Fame. Only thirty-nine names obtained a majority of votes, these being taken, of course, from men of all pursuits; and among these Longfellow ranked tenth, having eighty-five votes, and being preceded only by Washington, Lincoln,

Webster, Franklin, Grant, Marshall, Jefferson, Emerson, and Fulton. Besides Emerson and Longfellow, only two literary men were included, these being Irving with eighty-four votes and Hawthorne with seventy-three.

It is a well-known fact that when the temporary leader in any particular branch of literature or science passes away, there is often visible a slight reaction, perhaps in the interest of supposed justice, when people try to convince themselves that his fame has already diminished. Such reactions have notably occurred, for instance, in the cases of Scott, Byron, Wordsworth, and even of Burns, yet without visible or permanent results, while the weaker fame of Southey or of Campbell has yielded to them. It is safe to say that up to the present moment no serious visible reaction has occurred in the case of Longfellow. So absolutely simple and truthful was his nature and so clear the response of the mass of readers, that time has so far left his hold upon them singularly unaffected. During a recent visit to England, the author of this volume took some pains, in every place he visited in city or country, to inquire of the local bookseller as to the demand for Longfellow's poems, and the answer was always in substance and sometimes in express words, "He is a classic,"--in other words, his books had a steady and trustworthy sale. I always found his poems on the shelves, and this was true of no other American poet. Several editions of his works, single or collective, had recently appeared in London. Poems newly set to music had lately been published at the music stalls, and familiar citations from his poems were constantly heard in public speeches. Inquiries similar to mine were made a few years since in the book-stores of Switzerland and Germany by my friend, Professor W. J. Rolfe, who found without difficulty the German and English text of single or collected poems by Longfellow at Nuremberg, Cologne, Strasburg, Lucerne, Interlaken, and elsewhere.

Another form of obtaining statistics bearing on the relative position of Longfellow among English-writing poets would be to inspect books of selections made in Great Britain out of this class. I find two such lying near at hand; the first is "Pen and Pencil Pictures from the Poets," published by William P. Nimmo at Edinburgh, containing fifty-six poems in all, each with a full-page illustration, generally by Scottish artists. Of these selections, six are taken from Longfellow, five each from Wordsworth and Thomson, and three each from Shakespeare, Burns, and Moore. Of other American poets Bryant and Willis alone appear, each with one contribution. Another such book is

"Words from the Poets; selected for the use of parochial schools and libraries." To this the leading contributors are Wordsworth (twenty-one), Longfellow (eighteen), Cowper (eleven), and Tennyson (nine), the whole number of contributors being forty-three. Such statistics could be easily multiplied; indeed, it will be readily admitted that no American poet can be compared to Longfellow in the place occupied by his poems in the English market. Readily admitting that this is not the sole or highest standard, it must at least be recognized as one of the side tests by which that standard may be determined.

Some occasional expressions of distrust as to Longfellow's permanent fame have been based wholly upon his virtues. Many still cling to Dryden's maxim, "Great wits are sure to madness near allied." Those who grew up during the period when the Lake poets of England were still under discussion can well recall that the typical poet was long supposed to be necessarily something of a reprobate, or at any rate wild and untamable; so that Byron and Shelley gained in fame by the supposition that the domestic and law-abiding gifts were far from them. The prominence of Wordsworth was developed in spite of this tradition, and even when the report cheered some of his would-be admirers that he had once been intoxicated at the university, it was damped by the opinion expressed by Theodore Hook that "Wordsworth's conceptions of inebriation were no doubt extremely limited." The popular impression in such matters is too deep to be easily removed; and yet every test continues to prove that the hold taken on the average human heart by Longfellow is far greater than that held, for instance, by Poe or Whitman. This was practically conceded by those poets themselves, and it is this fact which in reality excited the wrath of their especial admirers. No man ever sacrificed less for mere fame than Longfellow, no man ever bore attack or jealousy with more of manly self-respect and sweetness; he simply lived his own life, and worked out his own literary method; all that he asked was to be taken for what he was worth, and the world's praise was the answer to his request. The continuance of this hold on men surely affords a sufficient reason for the renewed study of this poet's life, training, and career.

{1 N. Y. Independent, October 22, 1896.}

CHAPTER II

BIRTH, CHILDHOOD, AND YOUTH

Henry Wadsworth Longfellow was born in Portland, Maine, February 27, 1807, being the son of Stephen and Zilpah (Wadsworth) Longfellow, both his parents having been descended from Yorkshire families which had migrated in the seventeenth century. The name of Longfellow first appears in English records as Langfellay, while the name of Wadsworth sometimes appears as Wordsworth, suggesting a possible connection with another poet. His father, Stephen Longfellow, was a graduate of Harvard College in 1794, being a classmate of the Rev. Dr. W. E. Channing and the Hon. Joseph Story. He became afterward a prominent lawyer in Portland. He was also at different times a member of the Massachusetts Legislature, Maine being then a part of that State; a member of the celebrated "Hartford Convention" of Federalists; a presidential elector, and a member of Congress. In earlier generations the poet's grandfather was a judge of the Court of Common Pleas; his great-grandfather was a graduate of Harvard College in 1742, and was afterward town schoolmaster, parish clerk, and register of probate; his great-great-grandfather was a "village blacksmith;" and his ancestor once more removed, the American founder of the family, was William Longfellow, who was born in Hampshire County, England, in 1651, and came in early life to this country, where he engaged in mercantile pursuits. Thus much for the paternal ancestry.

To turn to the "spindle side," Mr. Longfellow's mother was Zilpah Wadsworth, eldest daughter of General Peleg Wadsworth, who was the son of Deacon Peleg Wadsworth, of Duxbury, Mass., and was the fifth in descent from Christopher Wadsworth, who came from England and settled in that town before 1632. The Peleg Wadsworth of military fame was born at Duxbury, and graduated from Harvard in 1769; he afterward taught school at Plymouth, and married Elizabeth Bartlett of that town; he then took part in the Revolution as captain of a company of minutemen, and rose to a major-general's command, serving chiefly on the eastern frontier. He was captured, was imprisoned, escaped, and had many stirring adventures. When the war was over he purchased from the State no less than 7500 acres of wild land, and spent the rest of his life at Hiram, Maine, representing his congressional district, however, for fourteen years in the national Congress. Through the Wadsworths and Bartletts, the poet could trace his descent to not less than four of the Mayflower pilgrims, including Elder Brewster and Captain John

Alden.

Judge Longfellow, the poet's grandfather, is described as having been "a fine-looking gentleman with the bearing of the old school; an erect, portly figure, rather tall; wearing, almost to the close of his life, the old-style dress,-- long skirted waistcoat, small-clothes, and white-topped boots, his hair tied behind in a club, with black ribbon." General Wadsworth was described by his daughter as "a man of middle size, well proportioned, with a military air, and who carried himself so truly that men thought him tall. His dress a bright scarlet coat, buff small-clothes and vest, full ruffled bosom, ruffles over the hands, white stockings, shoes with silver buckles, white cravat with bow in front, hair well powdered and tied behind in a club, so called." The poet was eminently well descended, both on the father's and mother's side, according to the simple provincial standard of those days.

Stephen Longfellow and his young wife lived for a time in a brick house built by General Wadsworth in Portland, and still known as "the Longfellow house;" but it was during a temporary residence of the family at the house of Samuel Stephenson, whose wife was a sister of Stephen Longfellow, that Henry Wadsworth Longfellow was born. He was the second son, and was named for an uncle, Henry Wadsworth, a young naval lieutenant, who was killed in 1804 by the explosion of a fire-ship, before the walls of Tripoli. The Portland of 1807 was, according to Dr. Dwight,--who served as a sort of travelling inspector of the New England towns of that period,--"beautiful and brilliant;" but the blight of the Embargo soon fell upon it. The town needed maritime defences in the war of 1812, and a sea-fight took place off the coast, the British brig Boxer being captured during the contest by the Enterprise, and brought into Portland harbor in 1813. All this is beautifully chronicled in the poem "My Lost Youth:"--

"I remember the sea-fight far away, How it thundered o'er the tide! And the dead captains, as they lay In their graves, o'erlooking the tranquil bay Where they in battle died. And the sound of that mournful song Goes through me with a thrill; 'A boy's will is the wind's will, And the thoughts of youth are long, long thoughts.'"

Here Henry Longfellow spent his childhood and youth. Much of that strong aversion to war which pervades the poet's verses may undoubtedly be charged to early association with his uncle's death.

The imaginative side of his temperament has commonly been attributed to his mother, who was fond of poetry and music, and a lover of nature in all its aspects; one who would sit by a window during a thunderstorm, as her youngest son has testified, "enjoying the excitement of its splendors." She loved the retirement of a country life, and found in it, in her own language, "a wonderful effect in tranquillizing the spirit and calming every unpleasant emotion." She played the spinet until her daughter's piano replaced it, and apparently read Cowper, Hannah More, and Ossian with her children. She sent them early to school, after the fashion of those days; this experience evidently beginning for Henry Longfellow at three years of age, when he went with a brother of five to a private school where he learned his letters. After several experiments, he was transferred, at the tolerably early age of six, to the Portland Academy. At this age, his teacher, Mr. Carter, wrote of him, "Master Henry Longfellow is one of the best boys we have in school. He spells and reads very well. He also can add and multiply numbers. His conduct last quarter was very correct and amiable." He began early to rhyme, and the first poem of his composing which is known to be preserved in manuscript is entitled, "Venice, an Italian Song," and was dated Portland Academy, March 17, 1820, he being then barely thirteen. There appeared a little later, in the poets' corner of the Portland "Gazette," the following verses, which show curiously, at the very outset, that vibration between foreign themes and home themes which always marks his verse:--

THE BATTLE OF LOVELL'S POND

Cold, cold is the north wind and rude is the blast That sweeps like a hurricane loudly and fast, As it moans through the tall waving pines lone and drear, Sighs a requiem sad o'er the warrior's bier.

The war-whoop is still, and the savage's yell Has sunk into silence along the wild dell; The din of the battle, the tumult, is o'er, And the war-clarion's voice is now heard no more.

The warriors that fought for their country, and bled, Have sunk to their rest; the damp earth is their bed; No stone tells the place where their ashes repose, Nor points out the spot from the graves of their foes.

They died in their glory, surrounded by fame, And Victory's loud trump their death did proclaim; They are dead; but they live in each Patriot's breast, And their names are engraven on honor's bright crest.

These verses cannot be assigned to the domain of high art, most certainly, but they mark in this case the beginning of a career, and milestones are always interesting. It was Longfellow's first poem, and he chose an American subject. We know from him the circumstances of the reception of this youthful effort. When the morning paper arrived it was unfolded and read by his father, and no notice was taken of the effusion; but when, in the evening, the boy went with his father to the house of Judge Mellen, his father's friend, whose son Frederic was his own playmate, the talk turned upon poetry. The host took up the morning's "Gazette." "Did you see the piece in to-day's paper? Very stiff. Remarkably stiff; moreover, it is all borrowed, every word of it." No defence was offered. It is recorded that there were tears on the young boy's pillow that night.

The young Henry Longfellow went to various schools, as those of Mrs. Fellows and Mr. Carter, and the Portland Academy, then kept by Mr. Bezaleel Cushman, a Dartmouth College graduate. In 1821, he passed the entrance examinations of Bowdoin College, of which his father was a trustee. The college itself was but twenty years old, and Maine had only just become an independent State of the Union, so that there was a strong feeling of local pride in this young institution. Henry Longfellow's brother, Stephen, two years older than himself, passed the examinations with him, but perhaps it was on account of the younger brother's youth--he being only fourteen--that the boys remained a year longer at home, and did not go to Brunswick until the beginning of the Sophomore year. Henry's college life was studious and modest. He and Nathaniel Hawthorne were classmates, having been friends rather than intimates, and Hawthorne gives in his "Fanshawe" a tolerably graphic picture of the little rural college. Neither of the two youths cared much for field sports, but both of them were greatly given to miscellaneous reading; and both of them also spent a good deal of time in the woods of Brunswick, which were, and still are, beautiful. Longfellow pursued the appointed studies, read poetry, was fond of Irving, and also of books about the Indians, an experience which in later life yielded him advantage.

It is just possible that these books may have revived in him a regret expressed in one of his early college letters that he had not gone to West Point instead of Bowdoin,--some opportunity of appointment to the military school, perhaps through his uncle, General Wadsworth, having possibly been declined in his behalf.{2} It is curious indeed to reflect that had he made this different selection, he might have been known to fame simply as Major-General Longfellow.

Hon. J. W. Bradbury, another classmate, describes Henry Longfellow as having "a slight, erect figure, delicate complexion, and intelligent expression of countenance," and further adds: "He was always a gentleman in his deportment, and a model in his character and habits." Still another classmate, Rev. David Shepley, D. D., has since written of Longfellow's college course: "He gave urgent heed to all departments of study in the prescribed course, and excelled in them all; while his enthusiasm moved in the direction it has taken in subsequent life. His themes, felicitous translations of Horace, and occasional contributions to the press, drew marked attention to him, and led to the expectation that his would be an honorable literary career." He spent his vacations in Portland, where the society was always agreeable, and where the women, as one of his companions wrote, seemed to him "something enshrined and holy,--to be gazed at and talked with, and nothing further." In one winter vacation he spent a week in Boston and attended a ball given by Miss Emily Marshall, the most distinguished of Boston's historic belles, and further famous as having been the object of two printed sonnets, the one by Willis and the other by Percival. He wrote to his father that on this occasion he saw and danced with Miss Eustaphie, daughter of the Russian consul, of whom he says, "She is an exceedingly graceful and elegant dancer, and plays beautifully upon the pianoforte." He became so well acquainted in later days with foreign belles and beauties that it is interesting to imagine the impression made upon him at the age of twenty-one by this first social experience, especially in view of the fact that after his returning from Europe, he records of himself that he never danced, except with older ladies, to whom the attention might give pleasure.

{2 From a manuscript letter not dated as to year, but written, apparently, while he was a freshman.}

CHAPTER III

FIRST FLIGHTS IN AUTHORSHIP

It is interesting to know that twice, during his college days, Longfellow had occasion to show his essentially American feeling; first, in his plea for the Indians on an Exhibition Day, and again, more fully and deliberately, in his Commencement Oration on "Our Native Writers." On Exhibition Day,--a sort of minor Commencement,--he represented, in debate, an American Indian, while his opponent, James W. Bradbury, took the part of an English emigrant. The conclusion of the exercise summed up the whole, being as follows:--

"Emigrant.--Is it thus you should spurn all our offers of kindness, and glut your appetite with the blood of our countrymen, with no excuse but the mere pretence of retaliation? Shall the viper sting us and we not bruise his head? Shall we not only let your robberies and murders pass unpunished, but give you the possession of our very fireside, while the only arguments you offer are insolence and slaughter? Know ye, the land is ours until you will improve it. Go, tell your ungrateful comrades the world declares the spread of the white people at the expense of the red is the triumph of peace over violence. Tell them to cease their outrages upon the civilized world or but a few days and they shall be swept from the earth.

"Savage.--Alas! the sky is overcast with dark and blustering clouds. The rivers run with blood, but never, never will we suffer the grass to grow upon our war-path. And now I do remember that the Initiate prophet, in my earlier years, told from his dreams that all our race should fall like withered leaves when autumn strips the forest! Lo! I hear sighing and sobbing: 'tis the death-song of a mighty nation, the last requiem over the grave of the fallen."{3}

It is fair to conjecture that we may have in this boyish performance the very germ of "Hiawatha," and also to recall the still more youthful verses which appeared in the Portland "Gazette." He wrote in college not merely such verses, but some prose articles for the "American Monthly Magazine," edited in Philadelphia, by Dr. James McHenry, who in his letters praised the taste and talent shown in the article upon "Youth and Age." More important to the young poet, however, was his connection with a new semi-monthly periodical called the "United States Literary Gazette." This was published in Boston and New York simultaneously, having been founded by the late Theophilus

Parsons, but edited at that time by James G. Carter, of Boston, well known in connection with the history of public schools. Apparently Longfellow must have offered poems to the "Gazette" anonymously, for one of his classmates records that when he met Mr. Carter in Boston the editor asked with curiosity what young man sent him such fine poetry from Bowdoin College. A modest volume of "Miscellaneous Poems, selected from the 'United States Literary Gazette,'" appeared in 1826,--the year after Longfellow left college,--and it furnished by far the best exhibit of the national poetry up to that time. The authors represented were Bryant, Longfellow, Percival, Dawes, Mellen, and Jones; and it certainly offered a curious contrast to that equally characteristic volume of 1794, the "Columbian Muse," whose poets were Barlow, Trumbull, Freneau, Dwight, Humphreys, and a few others, not a single poem or poet being held in common by the two collections.

This was, however, only a volume of extracts, but it is the bound volumes of the "Gazette" itself--beginning with April 1, 1824--which most impress the student of early American literature. There will always be a charm in turning over the pages where one sees, again and again, the youthful poems of Bryant and of Longfellow placed side by side and often put together on the same page, the young undergraduate's effusions being always designated by his initials and Bryant's with a perhaps more dignified "B.," denoting one whose reputation was to a certain extent already established, so that a hint was sufficient. Bryant's poems, it must be owned, are in this case very much better or at least maturer than those of his youthful rival, and are preserved in his published works, while Longfellow's are mainly those which he himself dropped, though they are reprinted in the appendix to Mr. Scudder's "Cambridge" edition of his poems. We find thus in the "Literary Gazette," linked together on the same page, Longfellow's "Autumnal Nightfall" and Bryant's "Song of the Grecian Amazon;" Longfellow's "Italian Scenery" and Bryant's "To a Cloud;" Longfellow's "Lunatic Girl" and Bryant's "The Murdered Traveller."{4} How the older poet was impressed by the work of the younger we cannot tell, but it is noticeable that in editing a volume of selected American poetry not long after, he assigns to Longfellow, as will presently be seen, a very small space. It is to be remembered that Bryant had previously published in book form, in 1821, his earliest poems, and the "Literary Gazette" itself, in its very first number, had pronounced him the first "original poet formed on this side of the Atlantic." "Our pleasure was equalled by our surprise," it says, "when we took up Bryant's poems, listened to the uncommon melody of the versification, wondered at the writer's perfect command of language, and found that they were American poems." "Though the English critics say of him," it continues, "that their poets must look to their laurels now that such a competitor has entered the ring, yet, let him remember that a few jousts in the ring never established the reputation of a knight."{5} It is a curious fact that the difference in actual quantity of poetic production between the older and younger poets should thus have been unconsciously suggested by the editor when Longfellow was but seventeen.

With Bryant and Longfellow, it would therefore seem, the permanent poetic literature of the nation began. "The Rivulet" and "The Hymn of the Moravian Nuns" appeared in the "Gazette" collection, and have never disappeared from the poetic cyclopedias. The volume included fourteen of Longfellow's youthful effusions, only six of which he saw fit to preserve; dropping behind him, perhaps wisely, the "Dirge Over a Nameless Grave," "Thanksgiving," "The Angler's Song," "Autumnal Nightfall," "A Song of Savoy," "Italian Scenery," "The Venetian Gondolier," and "The Sea Diver." He himself says of those which he preserved that they were all written before the age of nineteen, and this is obvious from the very date of the volume. Even in the rejected poems the reader recognizes an easy command of the simpler forms of melody, and a quick though not profound feeling for external nature. Where he subsequently revises these poems, however, the changes are apt to be verbal only, and all evidently matters of the ear. Thus in reprinting "The Woods in Winter," he omits a single verse, the following:--

"On the gray maple's crusted bark Its tender shoots the hoarfrost nips; Whilst in the frozen fountain--hark! His piercing beak the bittern dips."

It shows the gradual development of the young poet's ear that he should have dropped this somewhat unmelodious verse. As a rule he wisely forbore the retouching of his early poems. He also contributed to the "Gazette" three articles in prose, quite in Irving's manner, including a few verses. All these attracted some attention at the time. Mr. Parsons, the proprietor of the magazine, was thoroughly convinced of the vigor and originality of the young man's mind, and informed him that one of his poems, "Autumnal Nightfall," had been attributed to Bryant, while his name was mentioned in the "Galaxy" on a level with that of Bryant and Percival. The leadership of Bryant was of course unquestioned at that period, and Longfellow many years after acknowledged to that poet his indebtedness, saying, "When I look back upon my early years, I cannot but smile to see how much in them is really yours. It was an involuntary imitation, which I most readily confess."

Still more interesting as a study in the "Literary Gazette" itself are three prose studies, distinctly after the manner of Irving, and headed by a very un-American title, "The Lay Monastery." There is a singular parallelism between this fanciful title and the similar transformation in verse, at about the same time, in the "Hymn of the Moravian Nuns" at the consecration of Pulaski's banner. As in that poem a plain Moravian sisterhood, who supported their house by needlework, gave us an imaginary scene amid a chancel with cowled heads, glimmering tapers, and mysterious aisles, so the solitary in this prose article leads us into the society of an old uncle whose countenance resembles that of Cosmo on the medallions of the Medici, who has been crossed in love, and who wears a brocade vest of faded damask, with large sprigs and roses. The author thus proceeds in his description of the imaginary uncle and the marvellous surroundings:--

"When my uncle beheld my childish admiration for his venerable black-letter tome, he fondly thought that he beheld the germ of an antique genius already shooting out within my mind, and from that day I became with him as a favored wine. Time has been long on the wing, and his affection for me grew in strength as I in years; until at length he has bequeathed to me the peculiar care of his library, which consists of a multitude of huge old volumes and some ancient and modern manuscripts. The apartment which contains this treasure is the cloister of my frequent and studious musings. It is a curious little chamber, in a remote corner of the house, finished all round with painted panellings, and boasting but one tall, narrow Venetian window, that lets in upon my studies a 'dim, religious light,' which is quite appropriate to them.

"Everything about that apartment is old and decaying. The table, of oak inlaid with maple, is worm-eaten and somewhat loose in the joints; the chairs are massive and curiously carved, but the sharper edges of the figures are breaking away; and the solemn line of portraits that cover the walls hang faded from black, melancholy frames, and declare their intention of soon leaving them forever. In a deep niche stands a heavy iron clock that rings the hours with hoarse and sullen voice; and opposite, in a similar niche, is deposited a gloomy figure in antique bronze. A recess, curtained with tapestry of faded green, has become the cemetery of departed genius, and, gathered in the embrace of this little sepulchre, the works of good and great men of ancient days are gradually mouldering away to dust again."{6}

In view of this essentially artificial and even boyish style, it is not strange that one of his compositions should have been thus declined by the eminently just and impartial editor of the "North American Review," Jared Sparks.

DEAR SIR,--I return the article you were so good as to send me. In many respects it has a good deal of merit, but on the whole I do not think it suited to the "Review." Many of the thoughts and reflections are good, but they want maturity and betray a young writer. The style, too, is a little ambitious, although not without occasional elegance. With more practice the author cannot fail to become a good writer; and perhaps my judgment in regard to this article would not agree with that of others whose opinion is to be respected; but, after all, you know, we editors have no other criterion than our own judgment.{7}

Nevertheless the young aspirant felt more and more strongly drawn to a literary life, and this found expression in his Commencement oration on "Our Native Writers." His brother and biographer, writing of this address in later years, says of it, "How interesting that [theme] could be made in seven minutes the reader may imagine," and he does not even reprint it; but it seems to me to be one of the most interesting landmarks in the author's early career, and to point directly towards all that followed.

OUR NATIVE WRITERS

To an American there is something endearing in the very sound,--Our Native Writers. Like the music of our native tongue, when heard in a foreign land, they have power to kindle up within him the tender memory of his home and fireside; and more than this, they foretell that whatever is noble and attractive in our national character will one day be associated with the sweet magic of Poetry. Is, then, our land to be indeed the land of song? Will it one day be rich in romantic associations? Will poetry, that hallows every scene,-- that renders every spot classical,--and pours out on all things the soul of its enthusiasm, breathe over it that enchantment, which lives in the isles of Greece, and is more than life amid the "woods, that wave o'er Delphi's steep"? Yes!--and palms are to be won by our native writers!--by those that have been nursed and brought up with us in the civil and religious freedom of our country. Already has a voice been lifted up in this land,--already a spirit and a love of literature are springing up in the shadow of our free political institutions.

But as yet we can boast of nothing farther than a first beginning of a national literature: a literature associated and linked in with the grand and beautiful scenery of our country,--with our institutions, our manners, our customs,--in a word, with all that has helped to form whatever there is peculiar to us, and to the land in which we live. We cannot yet throw off our literary allegiance to Old England, we cannot yet remove from our shelves every book which is not strictly and truly American. English literature is a great and glorious monument, built up by the master-spirits of old time, that had no peers, and rising bright and beautiful until its summit is hid in the mists of antiquity.

Of the many causes which have hitherto retarded the growth of polite literature in our country, I have not time to say much. The greatest, which now exists, is doubtless the want of that exclusive attention, which eminence in any profession so imperiously demands. Ours is an age and a country of great minds, though perhaps not of great endeavors. Poetry with us has never yet been anything but a pastime. The fault, however, is not so much that of our writers as of the prevalent modes of thinking which characterize our country and our times. We are a plain people, that have had nothing to do with the mere pleasures and luxuries of life: and hence there has sprung up within us a quick-sightedness to the failings of literary men, and an aversion to everything that is not practical, operative, and thoroughgoing. But if we would ever have a national literature, our native writers must be patronized. Whatever there may be in letters, over which time shall have no power, must be "born of great endeavors," and those endeavors are the offspring of liberal patronage. Putting off, then, what Shakespeare calls "the visage of the times,"--we must become hearty well-wishers to our native authors:--and with them there must be a deep and thorough conviction of the glory of their calling,--an utter abandonment of everything else,--and a noble self-devotion to the cause of literature. We have indeed much to hope from these things;--for our hearts are already growing warm towards literary adventurers, and a generous spirit has gone abroad in our land, which shall liberalize and enlighten.

In the vanity of scholarship, England has reproached us that we have no finished scholars. But there is reason for believing that men of mere learning--men of sober research and studied correctness--do not give to a nation its great name. Our very poverty in this respect will have a tendency to give a national character to our literature. Our writers will not be constantly toiling and panting after classical allusions to the Vale of Tempe and the Etrurian river, nor to the Roman fountains shall--

"The emulous nations of the West repair To kindle their quenched urns, and drink fresh spirit there."

We are thus thrown upon ourselves: and thus shall our native hills become renowned in song, like those of Greece and Italy. Every rock shall become a chronicle of storied allusions; and the tomb of the Indian prophet be as hallowed as the sepulchres of ancient kings, or the damp vault and perpetual lamp of the Saracen monarch.

Having briefly mentioned one circumstance which is retarding us in the way of our literary prosperity, I shall now mention one from which we may hope a happy and glorious issue: It is the influence of natural scenery in forming the poetical character. Genius, to be sure, must be born with a man; and it is its high prerogative to be free, limitless, irrepressible. Yet how is it moulded by the plastic hand of Nature! how are its attributes shaped and modulated, when a genius like Canova's failed in the bust of the Corsican, and amid the splendor of the French metropolis languished for the sunny skies and vine-clad hills of Italy? Men may talk of sitting down in the calm and quiet of their libraries, and of forgetting, in the eloquent companionship of books, all the vain cares that beset them in the crowded thoroughfares of life; but, after all, there is nothing which so frees us from the turbulent ambition and bustle of the world, nothing which so fills the mind with great and glowing conceptions, and at the same time so warms the heart with love and tenderness, as a frequent and close communion with natural scenery. The scenery of our own country, too, so rich as it is in everything beautiful and magnificent, and so full of quiet loveliness or of sublime and solitary awe, has for our eyes enchantment, for our ears an impressive and unutterable eloquence. Its language is in high mountains, and in the pleasant valleys scooped out between them, in the garniture which the fields put on, and in the blue lake asleep in the hollow of the hills. There is an inspiration, too, in the rich sky that "brightens and purples" o'er our earth, when lighted up with the splendor of morning, or when the garment of the clouds comes over the setting sun.

Our poetry is not in books alone. It is in the hearts of those men, whose love for the world's gain,--for its business and its holiday,--has grown cold within them, and who have gone into the retirements of Nature, and have found there that sweet sentiment and pure devotion of feeling can spring up and live in the shadow of a low and quiet life, and amid those that have no splendor in their joys, and no parade in their griefs.

Thus shall the mind take color from things around us,--from them shall there be a genuine birth of enthusiasm,--a rich development of poetic feeling, that shall break forth in song. Though the works of art must grow old and perish away from earth, the forms of nature shall keep forever their power over the human mind, and have their influence upon the literature of a people.

We may rejoice, then, in the hope of beauty and sublimity in our national literature, for no people are richer than we are in the treasures of nature. And well may each of us feel a glorious and high-minded pride in saying, as he looks on the hills and vales,--on the woods and waters of New England,--

"This is my own, my native land."{8}

{3 Every Other Saturday, i. 21.}

{4 United States Literary Gazette, i. 237, 267, 286.}

{5 Literary Gazette, i. 8.}

{6 United States Literary Gazette, i. 348.}

{7 Life, i. 60.}

{8 First printed from the original MS. in Every Other Saturday, i. 116.}

CHAPTER IV

LITERATURE AS A PURSUIT

Longfellow graduated at Bowdoin College in June, 1825. There was in his mind, apparently, from the first, that definiteness of purpose which is so often wanting when a student takes his first college degree. There was for him no doubt or hesitation: it must be literature or nothing; and this not merely from a preference for the pursuit, but from an ambition, willingly acknowledged, to make a name in that direction. He writes to his friend, George W. Wells, "Somehow, and yet I hardly know why, I am unwilling to study any profession. I cannot make a lawyer of any eminence, because I have not a talent for argument; I am not good enough for a minister,--and as to physic, I utterly and absolutely detest it." Even a year before this, he had written to his father a letter of some moment, dated March 13, 1824, containing the following ominous passage: "I am curious to know what you do intend to make of me,--whether I am to study a profession or not; and if so, what profession. I hope your ideas upon this subject will agree with mine, for I have a particular and strong prejudice for one course of life, to which you, I fear, will not agree. It will not be worth while for me to mention what this is until I become more acquainted with your own wishes."{9}

This letter remaining for some months unanswered, there followed another which at last stated his own personal desire. It was written to his father and dated December 5, 1824.

"I take this early opportunity to write to you, because I wish to know fully your inclination with regard to the profession I am to pursue when I leave college.

"For my part I have already hinted to you what would best please me. I want to spend one year at Cambridge for the purpose of reading history and of becoming familiar with the best authors in polite literature; whilst at the same time I can be acquiring a knowledge of the Italian language, without an acquaintance with which I shall be shut out from one of the most beautiful departments of letters. The French I mean to understand pretty thoroughly before I leave college. After leaving Cambridge I would attach myself to some literary periodical publication, by which I could maintain myself and still enjoy the advantages of reading. Now, I do not think that there is anything visionary or chimerical in my plan thus far. The fact is--and I will not disguise it in the least, for I think I ought not--the fact is, I most eagerly aspire after future eminence in literature; my whole soul burns most ardently for it, and every earthly thought centres in it. There may be something visionary in this, but I flatter myself that I have prudence enough to keep my enthusiasm from defeating its own object by too great haste. Surely there never was a better opportunity offered for the exertion of literary talent in our own country than is now offered. To be sure, most of our literary men thus far have not been professedly so until they have studied and entered the practice of Theology, Law, or Medicine. But this is evidently lost time. I do believe that we ought to pay more attention to the opinion of philosophers, that 'nothing but Nature can qualify a man for knowledge.'

"Whether Nature has given me any capacity for knowledge or not, she has at any rate given me a very strong predilection for literary pursuits, and I am almost confident in believing that, if I can ever rise in the world, it must be by the exercise of my talent in the wide field of literature. With such a belief, I must say that I am unwilling to engage in the study of law."

Again on December 31 he writes to his father, by way of New Year's gift, "Let me reside one year at Cambridge; let me study belles-lettres, and after that time it will not require a spirit of prophecy to predict with some degree of certainty what kind of a figure I could make in the literary world. If I fail here, there is still time enough left for the study of a profession; and while residing at Cambridge, I shall have acquired the knowledge of some foreign languages which will be, through life, of the greatest utility."

The answer of the father is too characteristic to be omitted, whether for its views as to personal standards or as to poetic structure. Most youthful poets of that day had to face a critical method based strictly upon the versification of Pope, and their parents regarded all more flowing measures as having a slight flavor of the French Revolution.

"The subject of your first letter is one of deep interest and demands great consideration. A literary life, to one who has the means of support, must be very pleasant. But there is not wealth enough in this country to afford encouragement and patronage to merely literary men. And as you have not had the fortune (I will not say whether good or ill) to be born rich, you must adopt a profession which will afford you subsistence as well as reputation. I am happy to observe that my ambition has never been to accumulate wealth for my children, but to cultivate their minds in the best possible manner, and to imbue them with correct moral, political, and religious principles,-- believing that a person thus educated will with proper diligence be certain of attaining all the wealth which is necessary to happiness. With regard to your spending a year at Cambridge, I have always thought it might be beneficial; and if my health should not be impaired and my finances should allow, I should be very happy to gratify you.... In the 'Advertiser' of the 18th, I observe some poetry from the 'U. S. Literary Gazette,' which from the signature, I presume to be from your pen. It is a very pretty production, and I read it with pleasure. But you will observe that the second line of the sixth verse has too many feet. 'Beneath the dark and motionless beech.' I think it would be improved by substituting lonely for motionless. I suggest this for your consideration. I have the pleasure of hearing frequently from home. They complain that they have not heard a word from you since you left. This is unpardonable."

On January 24, 1825, the son wrote to his father again:--

"From the general tenor of your last letter it seems to be your fixed desire that I should choose the profession of the law for the business of my life. I am very much rejoiced that you accede so readily to my proposition of studying general literature for one year at Cambridge. My grand object in doing this will be to gain as perfect a knowledge of the French and Italian languages as can be gained without travelling in France and Italy,--though, to tell the truth, I intend to visit both before I die.... I am afraid you begin to think me rather chimerical in many of my ideas, and that I am ambitious of becoming a 'rara avis in terris.' But you must acknowledge the usefulness of aiming high,--at something which it is impossible to overshoot--perhaps to reach. The fact is, I have a most voracious appetite for knowledge. To its acquisition I will sacrifice everything.... Nothing delights me more than reading and writing. And nothing could induce me to relinquish the pleasures of literature, little as I have yet tasted them. Of the three professions I should prefer the law. I am far from being a fluent speaker, but practice must serve as a talisman where talent is wanting. I can be a lawyer. This will support my real existence, literature an ideal one.

"I purchased last evening a beautiful pocket edition of Sir William Jones's Letters, and have just finished reading them. Eight languages he was critically versed in; eight more he read with a dictionary; and there were twelve more not wholly unknown to him. I have somewhere seen or heard the observation that as many languages as a person acquires, so many times is he a man."{10}

It was undoubtedly an important fact to the young poet to be brought thus early in contact with Sir William Jones and his twenty-eight languages. It is the experience of all that the gift of learning a variety of tongues is something which peculiarly belongs to youth. In Southern Europe, in Russia, in the East, it is a common thing to encounter mere children who with next to no schooling will prattle readily in three or four languages with equal inaccuracy but with equal ease; while a much older person may acquire them by laborious study and yet never feel at home. One can hardly doubt Longfellow's natural readiness in that direction; he was always being complimented, at any rate--though this may not count for much--upon his aptness in pronouncing foreign tongues, and the ease with which his own compositions lent themselves to translation may very possibly have some obscure connection with his own gifts in this respect. His college training can have had little bearing upon it, since there is no evidence that his classmate Hawthorne, doubtless a man of higher genius, showed any such capacity.

{9 Life, i. 50.}

{10 Life, i. 57, 58.}

CHAPTER V

FIRST VISIT TO EUROPE

Longfellow's college class (1825) numbered thirty-seven, and his rank in it at graduation was nominally fourth--though actually third, through the sudden death of a classmate just before Commencement. Soon after his graduation, an opportunity occurred to establish a professorship of modern languages in the college upon a fund given by Mrs. Bowdoin; and he, being then scarcely nineteen, and nominally a law student in his father's office, was sent to Europe to prepare himself for this chair, apparently on an allowance of six hundred dollars a year. The college tradition is that this appointment--which undoubtedly determined the literary tendencies of his whole life--was given to him in consequence of the impression made upon an examining committee by the manner in which he had translated one of Horace's odes. He accordingly sailed from New York for Europe on May 15, 1826, having stopped at Boston on the way, where he dined with Professor George Ticknor, then holding the professorship at Harvard College to which Longfellow was destined to succeed at a later day. Professor Ticknor had himself recently returned from a German university, and urged the young man to begin his studies there, giving him letters of introduction to Professor Eichhorn, to Robert Southey, and to Washington Irving, then in Europe.

He sailed on the ship Cadmus, Captain Allen, and wrote to his mother from Havre that his passage of thirty days had been a dreary blank, and that the voyage was very tiresome because of the continual talking of French and broken English, adding, "For Frenchmen, you know, talk incessantly, and we had at least a dozen of them with us." In spite of this rather fatiguing opportunity, he was not at once at home in French, but wrote ere long, "I am coming on famously, I assure you." He wrote from Auteuil, where he soon went, "Attached to the house is an extensive garden, full of fruit-trees, and bowers, and alcoves, where the boarders ramble and talk from morning till night. This makes the situation an excellent one for me; I can at any time hear French conversation,--for the French are always talking. Besides, the conversation is the purest of French, inasmuch as persons from the highest circles in Paris are residing here,--amongst others, an old gentleman who was of the household of Louis the Sixteenth, and a Madame de Sailly, daughter of a celebrated advocate named Berryer, who was the defender of Marshal Ney in his impeachment for treason. There is also a young student of law here, who is my almost constant companion, and who corrects all my mistakes in speaking or writing the French. As he is not much older than I am, I do not feel so much embarrassed in speaking to him as I do in speaking to others. These are some of the advantages which I enjoy here, and you can easily imagine others which a country residence offers over that of a city, during the vacation of the literary institutions at Paris and the cessation of their lectures."

It is to be noticed from the outset that the French villages disappointed him as they disappoint many others. In his letters he recalls "how fresh and cheerful and breezy a New England village is; how marked its features--so different from the town, so peculiar, so delightful." He finds a French village, on the other hand, to be like a deserted town, having "the same paved streets, the same dark, narrow alleys without sidewalks, the same dingy stone houses, each peeping into its neighbor's windows, the same eternal stone walls, shutting in from the eye of the stranger all the beauty of the place and opposing an inhospitable barrier to the lover of natural scenery." But when he finds himself among rural scenes, he has the delight felt by many an American boy since his days, as in the picture following:--

"From Orleans I started on foot for Tours on the fifth of October. October is my favorite month of the twelve. When I reflected that if I remained in Paris I should lose the only opportunity I might ever enjoy of seeing the centre of France in all the glory of the vintage and the autumn, I 'shut the book-lid' and took wing, with a little knapsack on my back, and a blue cap,--not exactly like Quentin Durward, but perhaps a little more. More anon of him. I had gone as far as Orleans in the diligence because the route is through an uninteresting country.

"I began the pedestrian part of my journey on one of those dull, melancholy days which you will find uttering a mournful voice in Sewall's Almanack: 'Expect--much--rain--about--this--time!' 'Very miscellaneous weather, good for sundry purposes,'--but not for a journey on foot, thought I. But I had a merry heart, and it went merrily along all day. At sundown I found myself about seven leagues on my way and one beyond Beaugency. I found the route one continued vineyard. On each side of the road, as far as the eye could reach, there was nothing but vines, save here and there a glimpse of the Loire, the turrets of an old ch 鉳 eau, or spire of a village church. The clouds had passed away with the morning, and I had made a fine day's journey, cutting across the country, traversing vineyards, and living in all the luxury of thought which the occasion inspired. I recollect that at sunset I had entered a path which wound through a wide vineyard where the villagers were still at their labors, and I was loitering along, talking with the peasantry and searching for an auberge to pass the night in. I was presently overtaken by a band of villagers; I wished them a good evening, and finding that the girls of the party were going to a village at a short distance, I joined myself to the band. I wanted to get into one of the cottages, if possible, in order to study character. I had a flute in my knapsack, and I thought it would be very pretty to touch up at a cottage door, Goldsmith-like,--though I would not have done it for the world without an invitation. Well, before long, I determined to get an invitation, if possible. So I addressed the girl who was walking beside me, told her I had a flute in my sack, and asked her if she would like to dance. Now laugh long and loud! What do you suppose her answer was? She said she liked to dance, but she did not know what a flute was! What havoc that made among my romantic ideas! My quietus was made; I said no more about a flute, the whole journey through; and I thought nothing but starvation would drive me to strike up at the entrance of a village, as Goldsmith did."{11}

Thus, wherever he goes, his natural good spirits prevail over everything. Washington Irving, in his diary, speaks of Longfellow at Madrid as having "arrived safely and cheerily, having met with no robbers." Mrs. Alexander Everett, wife of the American minister at Madrid, writes back to America, "His countenance is itself a letter of recommendation." He went into good Spanish society and also danced in the streets on village holidays. At the Alhambra, he saw the refinement of beauty within the halls, and the clusters of gypsy caves in the hillside opposite. After eight months of Spain he went on to Italy, where he remained until December, and passed to Germany with the new year. He sums up his knowledge of the languages at this point by saying, "With the French and Spanish languages I am familiarly conversant so as to speak them correctly and write them with as much ease and fluency as I do the English. The Portuguese I read without difficulty. And with regard to my proficiency in the Italian, I have only to say that all at the hotel where I lodge took me for an Italian, until I told them I was an American." He settled down to his studies in Germany, his father having written, with foresight then unusual, "I consider the German language and literature much more important than the Italian." He did not, however, have any sense of actual transplantation, as is the case with some young students, for although he writes to his sister (March 28, 1829), "My poetic career is finished. Since I left America I have hardly put two lines together," yet he sends to Carey & Lea, the Philadelphia publishers, to propose a series of sketches and tales of New England life. These sketches, as given in his note-book, are as follows:--

"1. New England Scenery: description of Sebago Pond; rafting logs; tavern scene; a tale connected with the 'Images.'

"2. A New England Village: country squire; the parson; the little deacon; the farm-house kitchen.

"3. Husking Frolic: song and tales; fellow who plays the fife for the dance; tale of the Quoddy Indians; description of Sacobezon, their chief.

"5. Thanksgiving Day: its merry-making, and tales (also of the Indians).

"7. Description of the White Mountains: tale of the Bloody Hand.

"10. Reception of Lafayette in a country village.

"13. Down East: the missionary of Acadie."{12}

A few days after, he wrote from Gastingen to his father, "I shall never again be in Europe." We thus see his mind at work on American themes in Germany, as later on German themes in America, unconsciously predicting that mingling of the two influences which gave him his fame. His earlier books gave to studious Americans, as I can well recall, their first imaginative glimpses of Europe, while the poet's homeward-looking thoughts from Europe had shown the instinct which was to identify his later fame with purely American themes. It is to be noticed that whatever was artificial and foreign in Longfellow's work appeared before he went to Europe; and was the same sort of thing which appeared in all boyish American work at that period. It was then that in describing the Indian hunter he made the dance go round by the greenwood tree. He did not lay this aside at once after his return from Europe, and Margaret Fuller said of him, "He borrows incessantly and mixes what he borrows." Criticising the very prelude to "Voices of the Night," she pointed out the phrases "pentecost" and "bishop's-caps" as indications that he was not merely "musing upon many things," but on many books which described them. But the habit steadily diminished. His very gift at translation, in which he probably exceeded on the whole any other modern poet, led him, nevertheless, always to reproduce old forms rather than create new ones, thus aiding immensely his popularity with the mass of simple readers, while coming short of the full demands of the more critical. To construct his most difficult poems was thus mainly a serene pleasure, and something as far as possible from that conflict which kept Hawthorne all winter, by his wife's testimony, with "a knot in his forehead" while he was writing "The Scarlet Letter."

It is always to be borne in mind that, as Mr. Scudder has pointed out in his admirable paper on "Longfellow and his Art," the young poet was really preparing himself in Europe for his literary work as well as for his professional work, and half consciously. This is singularly confirmed by his lifelong friend, Professor George W. Greene, who, in dedicating his "The Life of Nathanael Greene" to his friend, thus recalls an evening spent together at Naples in 1828:--

"We wanted," he says, "to be alone, and yet to feel that there was life all around us. We went up to the flat roof of the house where, as we walked, we could look down into the crowded street, and out upon the wonderful bay, and across the bay to Ischia and Capri and Sorrento, and over the house-tops and villas and vineyards to Vesuvius. The ominous pillar of smoke hung suspended above the fatal mountain, reminding us of Pliny, its first and noblest victim. A golden vapor crowned the bold promontory of Sorrento, and we thought of Tasso. Capri was calmly sleeping, like a sea-bird upon the waters; and we seemed to hear the voice of Tacitus from across the gulf of eighteen centuries, telling us that the historian's pen is still powerful to absolve or to condemn long after the imperial sceptre has fallen from the withered hand. There, too, lay the native island of him whose daring mind conceived the fearful vengeance of the Sicilian Vespers. We did not yet know Niccolini; but his grand verses had already begun their work of regeneration in the Italian heart. Virgil's tomb was not far off. The spot consecrated by Sannazaro's ashes was near us. And over all, with a thrill like that of solemn music, fell the splendor of the Italian sunset."{13}

As an illustration of this obvious fact that Longfellow, during this first European visit, while nominally training himself for purely educational work, was fitting himself also for a literary career, we find from his letter to his father, May 15, 1829, that while hearing lectures in German and studying faithfully that language, he was, as he says, "writing a book, a kind of Sketch-Book of scenes in France, Spain, and Italy." We shall presently encounter this book under the name of "Outre-Mer." He connects his two aims by saying in the same letter, "One must write and write correctly, in order to teach." Again he adds, "The further I advance, the more I see to be done. The more, too, I am persuaded of the charlatanism of literary men. For the rest, my fervent wish is to return home." His brother tells us that among his note-books of that period, we find a favorite passage from Locke which reappears many years after in one of his letters and in his impromptu address to the children of Cambridge, in 1880: "Thus the ideas as well as the children of our youth often die before us, and our minds represent to us those tombs to which we are approaching; where, though the brass and marble remain, yet the inscriptions are effaced by time, and the imagery moulders away."{14} He also included a quotation from John Lyly's "Endymion," which ten years later furnished the opening of his own "Hyperion." "Dost thou know what a poet is? Why, fool, a poet is as much as one should say--a poet." When we consider what he had just before written to his sister, it only furnishes another illustration of the fact, which needs no demonstration, that young authors do not always know themselves.

He reached home from Europe, after three years of absence, on August 11, 1829, looking toward Bowdoin College as his abode, and a professorship of modern languages as his future position. Up to this time, to be sure, the economical college had offered him only an instructorship. But he had shown at this point that quiet decision and firmness which marked him in all practical affairs, and which was not always quite approved by his more anxious father. In this case he carried his point, and he received on the 6th of September this simple record of proceedings from the college:--

"In the Board of Trustees of Bowdoin College, Sept. 1st, 1829: Mr. Henry W. Longfellow having declined to accept the office of instructor in modern languages.

"Voted, that we now proceed to the choice of a professor of modern languages.

"And Mr. H. W. Longfellow was chosen."

Thus briefly was the matter settled, and he was launched upon his life's career at the age of twenty-two. Of those who made up his circle of friends in later years, Holmes had just graduated from Harvard, Sumner was a Senior there, and Lowell was a schoolboy in Cambridge. Few American colleges had at that time special professors of modern languages, though George Ticknor had set a standard for them all. Longfellow had to prepare his own text-books--to translate "L'Homond's Grammar," to edit an excellent little volume of French "Proverbes Dramatiques," and a small Spanish Reader, "Novelas Espalas." He was also enlisted in a few matters outside, and drew up the outline of a prospectus for a girls' high school in Portland, such high schools being then almost as rare as professorships of modern languages. He was also librarian. He gave a course of lectures on French, Spanish, and Italian literature, but there seems to have been no reference to German, which had not then come forward into the place in American education which it now occupies. As to literature, he wrote to his friend, George W. Greene, "Since my return I have written one piece of poetry, but have not published a line. You need not be alarmed on that score. I am all prudence now, since I can form a more accurate judgment of the merit of poetry. If I ever publish a volume, it will be many years first." It was actually nine years. For the "North American Review" he wrote in April, 1831, an essay on "The Origin and Progress of the French Language." He afterwards sent similar papers to the same periodical upon the Italian and Spanish languages and literatures, each of these containing also original translations. Thus he entered on his career as a teacher, but another change in life also awaited him.

{11 Life, i. 90, 91.}

{12 Life, i. 165.}

{13 Scudder's Men and Letters, 28, 29.}

{14 Locke, Essay on the Human Understanding, bk. ii. ch. 10, "Of Retention."}

CHAPTER VI

MARRIAGE AND LIFE AT BRUNSWICK

It has been a source of regret to many that the memoirs of Longfellow, even when prepared by his brother, have given, perhaps necessarily, so little space to his early love and first marriage, facts which are apt to be, for a poet, the turning-points in his career. We know that this period in Lowell's life, for instance, brought what seemed almost a transformation of his nature, making an earnest reformer and patriot of a youth who had hitherto been little more than a brilliant and somewhat reckless boy. In Longfellow's serener nature there was no room for a change so marked, yet it is important to recognize that it brought with it a revival of that poetic tendency which had singularly subsided for a time after its early manifestation. He had written to his friend, George W. Greene, on June 27, 1830, that he had long ceased to attach any value to his early poems or even to think of them at all. Yet after about a year of married life, he began (December 1, 1832) the introduction to his Phi Beta Kappa poem, and during the following year published a volume of poetical translations from the Spanish; thus imitating Bryant, then in some ways his model, who had derived so much of his inspiration from the Spanish muse. It is not unreasonable to recognize something of his young wife's influence in this rekindling of poetic impulse, and it is pleasant, in examining the manuscript lectures delivered by him at Bowdoin College and still preserved there, to find them accompanied by pages of extracts, here and there, in her handwriting. It will therefore be interesting to make her acquaintance a little farther.

Mary Storer Potter was the second daughter of the Hon. Barrett Potter and Anne (Storer) Potter of Portland, neighbors and friends of the Longfellow family. She had been for a time a schoolmate of Henry Longfellow at the private school of Bezaleel Cushman in Portland; and it is the family tradition that on the young professor's returning to his native city after his three years' absence in Europe he saw her at church and was so struck with her appearance as to follow her home afterwards without venturing to accost her. On reaching his own house, however, he begged his sister to call with him at once at the Potter residence, and all the rest followed as in a novel. They were married September 14, 1831, she being then nineteen years of age, having been born on May 12, 1812, and he being twenty-four.

It was a period when Portland was somewhat celebrated for the beauty of its women; and indeed feminine beauty, at least in regard to coloring, seems somewhat developed, like the tints of garden flowers, by the neighborhood of the sea. An oil painting of Mrs. Longfellow is in my possession, taken in a costume said to have been selected by the young poet from one of the highly illustrated annuals so much in vogue at that day. She had dark hair and deep blue eyes, the latter still represented in some of her nieces, although she left no children. Something of her love of study and of her qualities of mind and heart are also thus represented in this younger generation. She had never learned Latin or Greek, her father disapproving of those studies for girls, but he had encouraged her in the love of mathematics, and there is among her papers a calculation of an eclipse.

She had been mainly educated at the school, then celebrated, of Miss Gushing in Hingham. "My first impression of her," wrote in later years the venerable professor, Alpheus Packard,--who was professor of Latin and Greek at Bowdoin at the time of her marriage,--"is of an attractive person, blooming in health and beauty, the graceful bride of a very attractive and elegant young man." Some books from her girlish library now lie before me, dingy and time-worn, with her name in varying handwriting from the early "Mary S. Potter" to the later "Mary S. P. Longfellow." They show many marked passages and here and there a quotation. The collection begins with Miss Edgeworth's "Harry and Lucy;" then follow somewhat abruptly "Sabbath Recreations," by Miss Emily Taylor, and "The Wreath, a selection of elegant poems from the best authors,"--these poems including the classics of that day, Beattie's "Minstrel," Blair's "Grave," Gray's "Elegy," Goldsmith's "Traveller," and some lighter measures from Campbell, Moore, and Burns. The sombre muse undoubtedly predominated, but on the whole the book was not so bad an elementary preparation for the training of a poet's wife. It is a touching accidental coincidence that one of the poems most emphatically marked is one of the few American poems in these volumes, Bryant's "Death of the Flowers," especially the last verse, which describes a woman who died in her youthful beauty. To these are added books of maturer counsel, as Miss Bowdler's "Poems and Essays," then reprinted from the sixteenth English edition, but now forgotten, and Mrs. Barbauld's "Legacy for Young Ladies," discussing beauty, fashion, botany, the uses of history, and especially including a somewhat elaborate essay on "female studies," on which, perhaps, Judge Potter founded his prohibition of the classics. Mrs. Barbauld lays down the rule that "the learned languages, the Greek especially, require a great deal more time than a young woman can conveniently spare. To the Latin," she adds, "there is not an equal objection ... and it will not," she thinks, "in the present state of things, excite either a smile or a stare in fashionable company." But she afterwards says, "French you are not only permitted to learn, but you are laid under the same necessity of acquiring it as your brother is of acquiring the Latin." Mrs. Barbauld's demands, however, are not extravagant, as she thinks that "a young person who reads French with ease, who is so well grounded as to write it grammatically, and has what I should call a good English pronunciation will by a short residence in France gain fluency and the accent." This "good English pronunciation" of French is still not unfamiliar to those acquainted with Anglicized or Americanized regions of Paris.

Among the maturer books of Mary Potter was Worcester's "Elements of History," then and now a clear and useful manual of its kind, and a little book called "The Literary Gem" (1827), which was an excellent companion or antidote for Worcester's History, as it included translations from the German imaginative writers just beginning to be known, Goethe, Richter, and Kaner, together with examples of that American literary school which grew up partly in imitation of the German, and of which the "Legend of Peter Rugg," by William Austin, is the only specimen now remembered. With this as a concluding volume, it will be seen that Mary Potter's mind had some fitting preparation for her husband's companionship, and that the influence of Bryant in poetry, and of Austin, the precursor of Hawthorne, in prose, may well have lodged in her mind the ambition, which was always making itself visible in her husband, towards the new work of creating an American literature. It is in this point of view that the young wife's mental training assumed a real importance in studying the atmosphere of Longfellow's early days. For the rest, she was described by her next-door neighbor in Brunswick, Miss Emeline Weld, as "a lovely woman in character and appearance, gentle, refined, and graceful, with an attractive manner that won all hearts."{15}

Longfellow's salary at Bowdoin College was eight hundred dollars, as professor of modern languages, with an additional hundred as librarian. From the beginning he took the lead among American teachers in this department, the difficulty among these being that they consisted of two classes,-- Americans imperfectly acquainted with Europe and foreigners as imperfectly known in America. Even in the selection of mere tutors the same trouble always existed, though partially diminished, as time went on, by those refugees from revolutionary excitements in Europe, especially from Germany and Italy, who were a real addition to our university circles. Even these were from their very conditions of arrival a somewhat impetuous and unmanageable class, and in American colleges--as later during the Civil War in the American army--the very circumstances of their training made them sometimes hard to control as subordinates. It was very fortunate, when they found, as in Longfellow, a well-trained American who could be placed over their heads.

There were also text-books and readers to be prepared and edited by the young professor, one of which, as I well remember, was of immense value to students, the "Proverbes Dramatiques," already mentioned, a collection of simple and readable plays, written in colloquial French, and a most valuable substitute for the previous Racine and Corneille, the use of which was like teaching classes to read out of Shakespeare. Thus full of simple and congenial work, Longfellow went to housekeeping with his young wife in a house still attractive under its rural elms, and thus described by him:--

"June 23 [1831]. I can almost fancy myself in Spain, the morning is so soft and beautiful. The tessellated shadow of the honeysuckle lies motionless upon my study floor, as if it were a figure in the carpet; and through the open window comes the fragrance of the wild brier and the mock orange. The birds are carolling in the trees, and their shadows flit across the window as they dart to and fro in the sunshine; while the murmur of the bee, the cooing of doves from the eaves, and the whirring of a little humming-bird that has its nest in the honeysuckle, send up a sound of joy to meet the rising sun."

{15 Every Other Saturday, i. 20.}

CHAPTER VII

THE CORNER STONE LAID

That the young professor rose very early for literary work, even in November, we know by his own letters, and we also know that he then as always took this work very seriously and earnestly. What his favorite employment was, we learn by a letter to his friend George W. Greene (March 9, 1833) about a book which he proposes to publish in parts, and concerning which he adds, "I find that it requires little courage to publish grammars and school-books; but in the department of fine writing--or attempts at fine writing--it requires vastly more." As a matter of fact, he had already published preliminary sketches of "Outre-Mer" in the "New England Magazine," a Boston periodical just undertaken, putting them under the rather inappropriate title of "The Schoolmaster," the first appearing in the number for July 18, 1831,{16} and the sixth and last in the number for February, 1833.{17} He writes to his sister (July 17, 1831), "I hereby send you a magazine for your amusement. I wrote 'The Schoolmaster' and the translation from Luis de Gongora."{18} It is worth mentioning that he adds, "Read 'The Late Joseph Natterstrom.' It is good." This was a story by William Austin, whose "Peter Rugg, the Missing Man," has just been mentioned as an early landmark of the period.{19} It is fair to say, however, that the critic of to-day can hardly see in these youthful pages any promise of the Longfellow of the future. The opening chapter, describing the author as a country schoolmaster, who plays with his boys in the afternoon, is only a bit of Irving diluted,--the later papers, "A Walk in Normandy," "The Village of Auteuil," etc., carrying the thing somewhat farther, but always in the same rather thin vein. Their quality of crudeness was altogether characteristic of the period, and although Holmes and Whittier tried their 'prentice hands with the best intentions in the same number of the "New England Magazine," they could not raise its level. We see in these compositions, as in the "Annuals" of that day, that although Hawthorne had begun with his style already formed, yet that of Longfellow was still immature. This remark does not, indeed, apply to a version of a French drinking song,{20} which exhibits something of his later knack at such renderings. There was at any rate some distinct maturity in the first number of "Outre-Mer," which appeared in 1835. A notice of this book in the London "Spectator" closed with this expression of judgment: "Either the author of the 'Sketch Book' has received a warning, or there are two Richmonds in the field."

Literary history hardly affords a better instance of the direct following of a model by a younger author than one can inspect by laying side by side a page of the first number of "Outre-Mer" and a page of the "Sketch Book," taking in each case the first American editions. Irving's books were printed by C. S. Van Winkle, New York, and Longfellow's by J. Griffin, Brunswick, Maine; the latter bearing the imprint of Hilliard, Gray & Co., Boston, and the former of the printer only. Yet the physical appearance of the two sets of books is almost identical; the typography, distribution into chapters, the interleaved titles of these chapters, and the prefix to each chapter of a little motto, often in a foreign language. It must be remembered that the "Sketch Book," like "Outre-Mer," was originally published in numbers; and besides all this the literary style of Longfellow's work was at this time so much like that of Irving that it is very hard at first to convince the eye that Irving is not responsible for all. Yet for some reason or other the early copies of the "Sketch Book" command no high price at auction, while at the recent sale of Mr. Arnold's collection in New York the two parts of "Outre-Mer" brought $310. The work is now so rare that the library of Harvard University has no copy of the second part, and only an imperfect copy of the first with several pages mutilated, but originally presented to Professor Felton by the author and bearing his autograph. As to style, it is unquestionable that in "Outre-Mer" we find Washington Irving frankly reproduced, while in "Hyperion" we are soon to see the development of a new literary ambition and of a more imaginative touch.

The early notices of "Outre-Mer" are written in real or assumed ignorance of the author's name and almost always with some reference to Irving. Thus there is a paper in the "North American Review" for October, 1834, by the Rev. O. W. B. Peabody, who says of the book that it is "obviously the production of a writer of talent and of cultivated taste, who has chosen to give to the public the results of his observation in foreign countries in the form of a series of tales and sketches." He continues, "It is a form which, as every reader knows, had been recommended by the high example and success of Mr. Irving.... It is not to be supposed that in adopting the form of Mr. Irving, the author has been guilty of any other imitation."{21} This may in some sense be true, and yet it is impossible to compare the two books without seeing that kind of assimilation which is only made more thorough by being unconscious. Longfellow, even thus early, brought out more picturesquely and vividly than Irving the charm exerted by the continent of Europe over the few Americans who were exploring it. What Irving did in this respect for England, Longfellow did for the continental nations. None of the first German students from America, Ticknor, Cogswell, Everett, or Bancroft, had been of imaginative temperament, and although their letters, as since printed,{22} revealed Germany to America as the land of learning, it yet remained for Longfellow to portray all Europe from the point of view of the pilgrim. When he went to England in 1835, as we shall see, he carried with him for English publication the two volumes of one of the earliest literary tributes paid by the New World to the Old, "Outre-Mer."

It is a curious fact that Mr. Samuel Longfellow, in his admirable memoir of his brother, omits all attempt to identify the stories by the latter which are mentioned as appearing in the annual called "The Token," published in Boston and edited by S. G. Goodrich. This annual was the first of a series undertaken in America, on the plan of similar volumes published under many names in England. It has a permanent value for literary historians in this country as containing many of Hawthorne's "Twice-Told Tales" in their original form, but often left anonymous, and sometimes signed only by his initial (H.). In the list of his own early publications given by Longfellow to George W. Greene under date of March 9, 1833, he includes, "7. In 'The Token' for 1832, a story.... 8. In the same, for 1833, a story." To identify the contributions thus affords a curious literary puzzle. The first named volume-- "The Token" for 1832--contains the tale of a domestic bereavement under the name of "The Indian Summer;" this has for a motto a passage from "The Maid's Tragedy," and the whole story is signed with the initial "L." This would seem naturally to suggest Longfellow, and is indeed almost conclusive. Yet curiously enough there is in the same volume a short poem called "La Doncella," translated from the Spanish and signed "L....," which is quite in the line of the Spanish versions he was then writing, although not included in Mr. Scudder's list of his juvenile or unacknowledged poems. To complicate the matter still farther, there is also a story called "David Whicher," dated Bowdoin College, June 1, 1831, this being a period when Longfellow was at work there, and yet this story is wholly remote in style from "The Indian Summer," being a rather rough and vernacular woodman's tale. Of the two, "The Indian Summer" seems altogether the more likely to be his work, and indeed bears a distinct likeness to the equally tragic tale of "Jacqueline" in "Outre-Mer,"--the one describing the funeral of a young girl in America, the other in Europe, both of them having been suggested, possibly, by the recent death of his own sister.

In the second volume of "The Token" (1833) the puzzle is yet greater, for though there are half a dozen stories without initials, or other clue to authorship, yet not one of them suggests Longfellow at all, or affords the slightest clue by which it can be connected with him, while on the other hand there is a poem occupying three pages and signed H. W. L., called "An Evening in Autumn." This was never included by him among his works, nor does it appear in the list of his juvenile poems and translations in the Appendix to Mr. Scudder's edition of his "Complete Poetical Works," yet the initials leave hardly a doubt that it was written by him. Why, then, was it not mentioned in this list sent to Mr. George W. Greene, or did he by a slip of the pen record it as a story and not as a poem? Perhaps no solution of this conundrum will ever be given, but it would form a valuable contribution to the record of his literary dawning. Judging from the evidence now given, the most probable hypothesis would seem to be that the two contributions which Longfellow meant to enumerate were the story called "An Indian Summer" in "The Token" for 1832, and a poem, not a story, in "The Token" for 1833. Even against this theory there is the objection to be made that the editor of "The Token," Samuel G. Goodrich, in his "Recollections of a Lifetime" (New York, 1856), after mentioning Longfellow casually, at the very end of his list of writers, says of him, "It is a curious fact that the latter, Longfellow, wrote prose, and at that period had shown neither a strong bias nor a particular talent for poetry." It is farther noticeable that in his index to this book, Mr. Goodrich does not find room for Longfellow's name at all.{23}

It is to be borne in mind that at the very time when Longfellow was writing these somewhat trivial contributions for "The Token," he was also engaged on an extended article for "The North American Review," which was a great advance upon all that he had before published. His previous papers had all been scholarly, but essentially academic. They had all lain in the same general direction with Ticknor's "History of Spanish Literature," and had shared its dryness. But when he wrote, at twenty-four, an article for "The North American Review" of January, 1832,{24} called "The Defence of Poetry," taking for his theme Sir Philip Sidney's "Defence of Poesy," just then republished in the "Library of the Old English Prose Writers," at Cambridge, Mass., it was in a manner a prediction of Emerson's oration, "The American Scholar," five years later. So truly stated were his premises that they are still valid and most important for consideration to-day, after seventy years have passed. It is thus that his appeal begins:--

... "With us, the spirit of the age is clamorous for utility,--for visible, tangible utility,--for bare, brawny, muscular utility. We would be roused to action by the voice of the populace, and the sounds of the crowded mart, and not 'lulled to sleep in shady idleness with poet's pastimes.' We are swallowed up in schemes for gain, and engrossed with contrivances for bodily enjoyments, as if this particle of dust were immortal,--as if the soul needed no aliment, and the mind no raiment. We glory in the extent of our territory, in our rapidly increasing population, in our agricultural privileges, and our commercial advantages.... We boast of the increase and extent of our physical strength, the sound of populous cities, breaking the silence and solitude of our Western territories,--plantations conquered from the forest, and gardens springing up in the wilderness. Yet the true glory of a nation consists not in the extent of its territory, the pomp of its forests, the majesty of its rivers, the height of its mountains and the beauty of its sky; but in the extent of its mental power,--the majesty of its intellect,--the height and depth and purity of its moral nature.... True greatness is the greatness of the mind;-- the true glory of a nation is moral and intellectual preeminence."{25}

"Not he alone," the poet boldly goes on, "does service to the State, whose wisdom guides her councils at home, nor he whose voice asserts her dignity abroad. A thousand little rills, springing up in the retired walks of life, go to swell the rushing tide of national glory and prosperity; and whoever in the solitude of his chamber, and by even a single effort of his mind, has added to the intellectual preeminence of his country, has not lived in vain, nor to himself alone."{26}

He goes on to argue, perhaps needlessly, in vindication of poetry for its own sake and for the way in which it combines itself with the history of the nation, and expresses the spirit of that nation. He then proceeds to a direct appeal in behalf of that very spirit. Addressing the poets of America he says, "To those of them who may honor us by reading our article, we would whisper this request,--that they should be more original, and withal more national. It seems every way important, that now, whilst we are forming our literature, we should make it as original, characteristic, and national as possible. To effect this, it is not necessary that the war-whoop should ring in every line, and every page be rife with scalps, tomahawks, and wampum. Shade of Tecumseh forbid!--The whole secret lies in Sidney's maxim,--'Look in thy heart and write.'"{27}

He then points out that while a national literature strictly includes "every mental effort made by the inhabitants of a country through the medium of the press," yet no literature can be national in the highest sense unless it "bears upon it the stamp of national character." This he illustrates by calling attention to certain local peculiarities of English poetry as compared with that of the southern nations of Europe. He gives examples to show that the English poets excel their rivals in their descriptions of morning and evening, this being due, he thinks, to their longer twilights in both directions. On the other hand, the greater dreaminess and more abundant figurative language of southern nations are qualities which he attributes to their soft, voluptuous climate, where the body lies at ease and suffers the dream fancy "to lose itself in idle reverie and give a form to the wind and a spirit to the shadow and the leaf." He then sums up his argument.

"We repeat, then, that we wish our native poets would give a more national character to their writings. In order to effect this, they have only to write more naturally, to write from their own feelings and impressions, from the influence of what they see around them, and not from any preconceived notions of what poetry ought to be, caught by reading many books and imitating many models. This is peculiarly true in descriptions of natural scenery. In these, let us have no more sky-larks and nightingales. For us they only warble in books. A painter might as well introduce an elephant or a rhinoceros into a New England landscape. [This comes, we must remember, from the young poet who had written in his "Angler's Song" six years before,--

"Upward speeds the morning lark To its silver cloud."]

We would not restrict our poets in the choice of their subjects, or the scenes of their story; but when they sing under an American sky, and describe a native landscape, let the description be graphic, as if it had been seen and not imagined. We wish, too, to see the figures and imagery of poetry a little more characteristic, as if drawn from nature and not from books. Of this we have constantly recurring examples in the language of our North American Indians. Our readers will all recollect the last words of Pushmataha, the Choctaw chief, who died at Washington in the year 1824: 'I shall die, but you will return to your brethren. As you go along the paths, you will see the flowers and hear the birds; but Pushmataha will see them and hear them no more. When you come to your home, they will ask you, where is Pushmataha? and you will say to them, He is no more. They will hear the tidings like the sound of the fall of a mighty oak in the stillness of the wood.' More attention on the part of our writers to these particulars would give a new and delightful expression to the face of our poetry. But the difficulty is, that instead of coming forward as bold, original thinkers, they have imbibed the degenerate spirit of modern English poetry."{28} What is meant by this last passage is seen when he goes on to point out that each little village then had "its little Byron, its self-tormenting scoffer at morality, its gloomy misanthropist in song," and that even Wordsworth, in some respects an antidote to Byron, was as yet "a very unsafe model for imitation;" and he farther points out "how invariably those who have imitated him have fallen into tedious mannerisms." He ends with a moral, perhaps rather tamely stated: "We hope, however, that ere long some one of our most gifted bards will throw his fetters off, and relying on himself alone, fathom the recesses of his own mind, and bring up rich pearls from the secret depths of thought."{29}

"The true glory of a nation"--this is his final attitude--"is moral and intellectual preeminence;" thus distinctly foreshadowing the title of his friend Charles Sumner's later oration, "The True Grandeur of Nations." American literature had undoubtedly begun to exist before this claim was made, as in the prose of Irving and Cooper, the poetry of Dana and Bryant. But it had awaited the arrival of some one to formulate its claims, and this it found in Longfellow.

{16 New England Magazine, i. 27.}

{17 Ibid. iv. 131.}

{18 MS. letter.}

{19 See Writings of William Austin, Boston, 1890.}

{20 New England Magazine, ii. 188.}

{21 North American Review, xxix. 459.}

{22 Harvard Graduates' Magazine, vi. 6.}

{23 Goodrich's Recollections of a Lifetime, ii. 263, 560.}

{24 North American Review, xxxiv. 56.}

{25 North American Review, xxxiv. 59.}

{26 North American Review, xxxiv. 61.}

{27 Ib. 69.}

{28 North American Review, xxxiv. 74, 75.}

{29 Ib. 78.}

CHAPTER VIII

APPOINTMENT AT HARVARD AND SECOND VISIT TO EUROPE

While he was thus occupied with thoughts and studies which proved to be more far-seeing than he knew, the young professor was embarrassed by financial difficulties in which the college found itself; and he began after three years to consider the possibility of a transfer to other scenes, perhaps to some professorship in New York or Virginia.

The following letter, hitherto unpublished, gives us the view taken in the Longfellow house of another project, namely, that of his succeeding to the charge of the then famous Round Hill School at Northampton, about to be abandoned by its projector, Joseph G. Cogswell. The quiet judgment of the young wife thus sums it up in writing to her sister-in-law:--

Sunday afternoon [February, 1834].

... Henry left us Friday noon in the mail for Boston, as George will tell you. I do not like the idea of his going to Northampton at all--although it would be a most beautiful place to reside in. Still I feel sure he would not like the care of a school, and such an extensive establishment as that is too. He heard that Mr. Cogswell was to leave them for Raleigh and wrote him--in answer to which he received a long letter, wishing him much to take the place, &c.; which determined him to go immediately to Northampton. He requires $1600 to be advanced, and it would be incurring a certain expense upon a great uncertainty of gaining more than a living there. I do not think Henry calculated at all for such a situation. If he dislikes so much the care of such a little family as ours, how can he expect to like the multifarious cares of such a large one! He has promised not to decide upon anything till he returns, and I feel so confident that all uninterested persons will dissuade him from it, that I rest quite at ease. I wished him to go to satisfy himself, he was so very sanguine as to the result of it. We expect him home the last of next week. This Northampton business is a profound secret and is not mentioned out of the family!

Another extract from the same correspondent shows us how Longfellow was temporarily influenced at Brunswick, like Lowell afterwards at Cambridge, by the marked hygienic and even ascetic atmosphere of the period; an influence apparently encouraged in both cases by their young wives, yet leaving no permanent trace upon the habits of either poet,--habits always moderate, in both cases, but never in the literal sense abstemious.

Friday evening [April, 1834].

... He has gone to a Temperance Lecture this evening. He intends becoming a member of the Temperance Society; indeed I do not know but he has signed the paper already. He is a good little dear, and I approve of everything (almost smoking) he does. He is becoming an advocate of vegetable diet, Dr. Mussey's hobby; and Clara and I have nothing but lectures from him and Alexander, upon corsets.

The following extract gives us a glimpse of his literary work:--

BRUNSWICK, Nov. 2, 1834.

Henry comes on famously with Outre Mer. The No. on Spain is finished and that on Italy will be before Thanksgiving. It is by far more interesting than any of the other No's. Henry thinks himself it is much superior in point of interest and in style. I presume he will have the remaining No's published together in N. Y. this winter.

In the midst of such literary and household cares he received the following letter:--

CAMBRIDGE, December 1, 1834.

DEAR SIR,--Professor Ticknor has given notice that it is his intention to resign his office of Smith Professor of Modern Languages in Harvard University, as soon as the Corporation shall have fixed upon a successor.

The duty of nominating to that office devolves upon me; and after great deliberation and inquiry my determination is made to nominate you for that office under circumstances which render your appointment not doubtful,-- provided I receive a previous assurance from you of your acceptance of it. To ascertain this is the object of the present letter.

The salary will be fifteen hundred dollars a year. Residence in Cambridge will be required. The duties of the professorship will be of course those which are required from the occupant of a full professorship, and such as the Corporation and the Overseers may appoint. If a relation such as I suggest with this university be acceptable to you, I shall be obliged by an early answer.

Should it be your wish, previously to entering upon the duties of the office, to reside in Europe, at your own expense, a year or eighteen months for the purpose of a more perfect attainment of the German, Mr. Ticknor will retain his office till your return.

Very respectfully, I am Yours, etc., etc.,

JOSIAH QUINCY.{30}

"Good fortune comes at last and I certainly shall not reject it," the young Longfellow wrote to his father. "The last paragraph of the letter," he adds, "though put in the form of a permission, seems to imply a request. I think I shall accept that also." Some additional correspondence, however, proved necessary, such as follows:--

HON. JOSIAH QUINCY:

SIR,--Your letter of to-day inclosing the Vote of the President and Fellows of Har'd University in relation to the Professorship of Mod'n Lang's has been received, and in expressing anew my desire to meet your wishes fully in the matter before us, I beg leave to defer an official answer until my return from the South, in about three weeks hence.

In the mean time may I take the liberty of calling your attention once more to the subject of our last conversation? I feel it important that I should be regularly appointed before sailing for Europe. Otherwise I present myself as any private individual whatever. But if I go as one of your professors, I carry with me in that very circumstance my best letter of recommendation. It gives me a character--and a greater claim to attention abroad, than I can otherwise take with me. Judge Story is ready to consent to this arrangement--so is Mr. Gray--so is Mr. Ticknor. If you could bring the subject once more before the corporation, I think the objections suggested by you when I saw you this morning will be found to give way before the good results, which I think may be reasonably anticipated from change in your vote where respectfully suggested.

Very respect'y y'r. Ob'e. Ser't.

HENRY W. LONGFELLOW.{31}

BOSTON, Jan'y 1, 1834. [Error for 1835.]

HON. JOSIAH QUINCY:

SIR,--Placing entire confidence in the assurances of the President and Fellows of Harvard University in reference to my election to the Smith Professorship of Modern Languages and Belles Lettres in that institution, which assurances were communicated to me in y'r favor of 1st January, together with their Vote upon the subject,--I have the honor to inform you, that I shall sail for Europe in the month of April next, and remain there till the summer of 1836.

Very respectfully

HENRY W. LONGFELLOW.{32}

PORTLAND, February 3, 1835.

His first book, in a strict sense, published before his departure, was his translation of the "Coplas of Jorge Manrique" (1833), in which were added to the main poem a few translations of sonnets, the whole being prefaced with an article from "The North American Review" on the "Moral and Devotional Poetry of Spain." It was these works which had attracted the attention of Professor Ticknor, and had led to results so important. The young professor sailed at the time mentioned, accompanied by his wife and two young ladies, her friends.

His first aim was Sweden, but he spent a few weeks in London, where he met, among others, Carlyle. So little has hitherto been recorded of this part of Longfellow's life or of his early married life in any way, that I am glad to be able to describe it from the original letters of the young wife, which are now in my possession, and are addressed mainly to Mrs. Longfellow, her mother-in-law. She seems to have enjoyed her travelling experiences very thoroughly, and writes in one case, "We are generally taken for French ... and I am always believed to be Henry's sister. They say to me, 'What a resemblance between your brother and self!'"

Sunday afternoon, May 31, 1835.

MY DEAR MOTHER,--I wrote you a very few lines, in great haste, in Henry's letter to his Father, acknowledging the receipt of your kind letter. I hope that you will write us as often as your many cares will permit, & be assured that even a few lines will always be welcomed with delight by your absent children. We have passed our time very delightfully in London. The only difficulty is--there is so much to be seen & so little time to see it in. We have, however, seen many of the principal points. Last Monday we passed very delightfully at Shirley Park, near the little village of Croydon. The ride is through a very beautiful country. We passed several gipsy encampments, in the most picturesque situations. Shirley Park is a truly delightful place. The house, which is a very fine one, is placed on a beautiful spot, & there are fine views from all sides of it. Mrs. Skinner, the lady of the place, is a very agreeable amiable lady--She took us all over the grounds in her carriage, & was very kind & attentive to us. Her house is thronged with visitors, the great, the fashionable, & the literati all pay their court to her. She is a great admirer of Willis's, & thinks his writings superior to Irving's!--On Wednesday we visited the National Gallery, the finest collection of old paintings in the city. We saw while we were there, the Queen pass into the city, attended by the horse-guards in their beautiful uniforms. Five or six carriages passed with a coachman & two footmen to each, lost almost in the quantity of gold lace which covered them. Last of all came her Majesty's carriage with two coachmen & four footmen in the same magnificent livery. Thursday was the king's birth day. The drawing room was the most splendid one that had ever been seen--so Willis says. In the eve'g there was a grand illumination. About ten Henry and Mr. Frazer went out to see it. The crowd was so immense, that it was with the greatest difficulty they made their way home. Four women from St. Giles's armed with large clubs pointed with iron, passed through the crowd striking in all directions. We took a carriage & drove to see the illuminations. It was after eleven & the crowd had nearly dispersed. There were brilliant crowns & a variety of pretty devices formed with coloured lamps & some very fine gas ones. I suspect however there was very little true rejoicing in all this show & splendour. The Queen is very unpopular among the people. Friday morn'g--Willis called. He had been to breakfast with the beautiful Mrs. Wadsworth, & was on his way, to breakfast at 3 in the aft. with the Duchess of St. Albans. Mrs. Wadsworth, from Genesseo, was a Philadelphia lady & has been greatly admired on the continent & here. She returns in a few days to America. Yesterday morning Mr. Barnard a young lawyer from Connecticut called upon me. He arrived but a month before us, & takes much the same route as we do, though a more extensive one. He will be in Stockholm in the course of the summer. Mr. Carlyle of Craigenputtock was soon after announced, & passed an half hour with us much to our delight. He has very unpolished manners, & broad Scottish accent, but such fine language & beautiful thoughts that it is truly delightful to listen to him. Perhaps you have read some of his articles in the Edinburgh Review. He invited us to take tea with him at Chelsea, where they now reside. We were as much charmed with Mrs. C[arlyle] as with her husband. She is a lovely woman with very simple & pleasing manners. She is also very talented & accomplished, & how delightful it is to see such modesty combined with such power to please. On Tuesday we visit Chantrey's study with them. This morning Mr. Bentham, a nephew of Jeremy's, called, & invited us to dine with them on Wednesday--We may see the great potentate appear. Henry is petitioning for room to write, & saying that I must retire, but I must tell you my dreams. A few nights since I heard Samuel [Longfellow] preach for Dr. Nichols. Last night I dreamt I was with my father & sisters, telling them of all I had seen. I only went to America to make a call & tell you all we had safely arrived, & was to return immediately. You will give very much love to all for me. They must all write me, & their letters shall be answered as speedily as possible. We leave here the last of this week. I shall leave letters to be sent by the first opportunity. George & Ann must not forget us.

Your ever affectionate

MARY.

The Carlyles are again mentioned in a letter written while crossing the German Ocean.

STEAM SHIP, GERMAN OCEAN, Thursday, June 11 [1835].

... We have some very pleasant passengers. A German lady with her father and little girl. What a strange idea foreigners have of America! This lady who appears very intelligent asked us if America was anything like London!! Then we have a German Prince with huge mustachios; Clara played whist with him last evening! Oh dear! I do not know as I shall be able to speak to you when I return, I see so many lords and ladies! but in reality these lords and ladies are not half as agreeable people as some of Henry's literary friends. Mr. and Mrs. Carlyle have more genuine worth and talent than half of the nobility in London. Mr. Carlyle's literary fame is very high, and she is a very talented woman--but they are people after my own heart--not the least pretension about them. Mrs. Carlyle has a pin with Goethe's head upon it, which that great author sent her himself. She is very proud of it I assure you. They live very retired, not wishing to mix with fashionable society, which they regard in its true light; still they have some friends among the nobility who know how to value them.

STOCKHOLM, August 5, 1835.

MY DEAR MOTHER,--I hope you have received my letter to you from London ere this. We sent letters home from here July 21st by Capt. Symons directly to Boston--it was as soon as possible after our arrival; among them Henry sent a letter to his father, & I to Mary, Sam & Anne. I was quite delighted to receive a letter from Mary & Sam--hope they will write me often. Since our last letters we have removed our lodgings to "No. 5. Clara Sara Kyko Gatan." We have more rooms but not as good ones as in the Droteninggatan. We have made some very pleasant acquaintances here. July 15th we dined at Mr. Arfwedson's--the father of the gentleman who married an American lady. Mr. A---- resides at Liston Hill in the Park--he has a little English cottage, built by Sir Robert Liston, formerly English minister to this court. It is a sweet spot-- the Muler flows almost directly beneath the windows of the cottage--a little flower garden is upon its banks, & a fine grove of trees in the rear of the cottage. Mr. Arfwedson is a fine old man--his wife has been dead several years. The only ladies present were our countrywoman Mrs. A---- & the eldest daughter of Mr. Arfwedson--the wife of Baron S----. She is a very delicate and graceful lady, was dressed very tastefully & altogether unlike the Swedish ladies we had before seen. Mr. A's second daughter is just married to a brother of her sister's husband who is also a Baron. They went immediately to Copenhagen, we have not therefore seen her, but have heard much of her great beauty. There were a number of gentlemen present at dinner, several of which were English. The dinner table was by far the prettiest we have seen in Sweden.... The dessert plates were very beautiful, white china--upon each of which was a different flower elegantly painted. After coffee the gentleman proposed a drive to Rosendale, a little palace in the park. It is the favorite spot of king Bernadotte. We first went to the splendid porphyry vase, which stands in the centre of the flower garden back of the palace. The top of this celebrated & immense vase is cut from a single block of porphyry. Sweden is very celebrated for its fine porphyry. The lower rooms of the palace are handsomely furnished, but the upper ones are quite splendid. All the rooms were carpeted with beautiful carpets--the walls were hung with silk damask-- each room a different color, with curtains, sofas & chairs to correspond. One room was hung with white damask, & the chairs & sofa were covered with beautiful embroidery--the ground of which was white, wrought by the Queen & her maids of honor. There was a great profusion of this beautiful embroidery--fire screens, ottomans, &c.--The chandeliers, mirrors & candelabras were very elegant. In one room was a portrait of the king, which was very like him. In another that of the Queen--much flattered. She was a daughter of a merchant of Marseilles. There are no bed-chambers in this palace. The king very rarely sleeps out of his palace in town. We returned to Mr. Arfwedson's & took tea. Mrs. A---- is very accomplished, she speaks nearly all the modern languages. She invited us to dine with them on the next Sabbath.

July 16th. We dined at Mr. Stockoe's, a partner of Mr. Erskine's. We met quite a large & pleasant party there. The Stockoe's are excellent, kind-hearted people. They have paid us every attention. Mrs. S---- sends us presents of fruits & flowers, & all those little attentions which it is so agreeable to receive.--I was quite unwell on Sunday, on account of a very long walk the evening previous. I did not therefore go to young Arfwedson's. Clara & H---- went & had a very pleasant visit. They met there Baron

Stackelberg, who was Swedish minister in America fourteen years. He returned but two years since. He has called upon us several times since, & is a jovial old man with perfectly white hair & whiskers. July 22nd. The Stockoe's invited us to drive out to Haga with them. We went out at six in the evening. This palace is about two English miles from town. It was built by Gustavus the 3rd, & was his favorite residence. The furniture was very old, but there is one fine room lined with mirrors. In the drawing room is a centre table with a deep top & pots of flowers placed in it. This top was covered entirely with moss, this had a very pretty effect, especially as there were a variety of flowers all in bloom. The table was on castors & could be placed in any position.... We were shown three very small chambers, where Gustavus the 4th was imprisoned after he was dethroned. His queen lived with him there. In another building, a pavilion, were some rooms furnished in more modern style. The Queen sleeps in these rooms when she comes to Haga, [but] the royal family rarely visit this palace. The grounds are very beautiful. We walked round the Park to the famous palace which Gustavus 3d commenced building after his return from Italy. Here he expended two millions, & the foundations were but laid & the stones in readiness for the walls when he was assassinated. The work was then immediately stopped as the people were much opposed to the undertaking. We saw the model of this building which was to have been a very extensive one. A row of columns all around it, to have been built in the Italian style. The model was more like a temple than a palace. We took tea at a little inn in Hagalund & returned home late in the evening--The king has a great number of palaces round Stockholm, there are seven or eight, & as many it is said in every province.

We have a very pleasant little family of our own, & have fine times together. Mr. Hughes says "for one lady it would have been intolerable, for two very unpleasant; but for three quite agreeable." Henry has been much disappointed not to receive a letter from his father. We are now expecting letters every day from home, & when Wm. Goddard arrives next month we hope to have many--

Please to give my love to Aunt Lucia & say to her I shall write her very soon. Be so kind as to give much love to all the family for me, & accept much love & respect for yourself & Mr Longfellow from

Your ever affectionate

MARY ----

MY DEAREST MOTHER,--As a little blank space is left, I will fill it with a postscript.--We have just returned--that is to say, day before yesterday,--from a visit to the University of Upsala, and the Iron mines of Dannemora;--of which Mary will give you a description all in good time. We already begin to think of leaving Stockholm--and shall probably take the steamboat to Gothenburg in about three weeks.--For my own part, I should like to go sooner if we could. I am disappointed in Sweden. The climate is too cold and unpleasant. I want a little warm sunshine. Something that I can feel, as well as see. From Gothenburg we shall go to Copenhagen, and after passing a month there, take steamboat to Stettin, and so to Berlin. We shall not return to the North again but pass the next summer in Germany and France.

Much love to all. Very affectionately your Son

H. W. LONGFELLOW

MRS. STEPHEN LONGFELLOW, Care of Hon. Stephen Longfellow, Portland, Maine, U. S. of America.

[TO] HON. STEPHEN LONGFELLOW, PORTLAND, MAINE, U. S. OF AMERICA.

COPENHAGEN, September 21, 1835.

MY DEAR SIR,--Henry has consented that I should copy a few pages of his journal for you; but I could not prevail on him to grant this, till I promised again & again for you, that you would not on any condition, allow it to go out of your house. The children can read it there; & I will ask of you the same favor for my father and my sisters, for I know they will take much interest in it.

If it cheers a lonely winter's evening, or cheats you of a few melancholy hours, I shall feel most amply repaid for the trouble I have taken.

We have regretted much to hear of your feeble health, but hope that your journey has quite renovated you. I [was] delighted to receive a second letter from Mrs. L[ongfellow], in a p[ackage] of letters which reached us a few days since. She is very kind to write me, & I shall not fail to write her, as often as possible, while absent.

With this you will receive a letter for Aunt Lucia. I shall answer Mrs. L's letter very soon.

Henry has become quite learned in the Swedish, & can already translate Danish. He is studying Icelandic also, as I presume he has told you. He is in fine health & spirits.

With many wishes for your health & my Mother's, & with much respect & affection for you both--I am as ever

Your affectionate

MARY ----

[On outside of letter.] September 28. I have written by the same ship that brings you this. H. W. L. Also a letter to George.

[Endorsement.] Mary P. Longfellow to S. Longfellow, containing a Copy of Henry's Journal Sept. 21, 1835.{33}

COPENHAGEN, September 22, 1835.

MY DEAR AUNT LUCIA,--Pray do not be alarmed on receiving this letter for fear that you must answer it. I have not hoped such a favor, but am content, however much I should be delighted to hear from you, to write you occasionally without the hopes of an answer, thinking & knowing you would be as happy to receive a letter from me as any of my dear friends. I received a very entertaining letter from Anne a few days since. Henry says "Anne's letters have some pith to them." Pray urge her to write us often, & I shall take just as much interest in hearing about her family affairs as if I was in Brunswick.

And so you have made a visit in Boston, & have been upon railroads, to balloon ascensions, theatres & I know not what. After such a quiet life as you have passed for several years, it must be quite a pleasant little incident, & I know that you must have enjoyed your visit much. But, after all, do you not think that the pleasure of travelling is greatest when it has been all passed, & you are seated once more in your quiet home,--& retrace in imagination your wanderings? It must be so--I think--then you remember only what is agreeable, & the thousand little inconveniences, one must suffer in travelling, are forgotten.

I cannot tell you how delighted we all are that we are out of Sweden. Henry scolds not a little that a summer in Europe should have been passed there.

You have heard before this, by our letters from Gothenburg, that we were detained there a week, much against our will. We passed the time, however, very pleasantly. H[enry] delivered a letter from my Uncle Robert [Storer] to Mr. Wijk of that place, & he was very attentive & kind to us. On Sunday the 6th of September we dined with him, & had the pleasure of being introduced to his celebrated lady. She appears as his daughter, being more than thirty years younger than her husband. We had heard of her great beauty in America. I cannot say that she is beautiful, but she is extremely pretty with very interesting manners. They have travelled much on the continent & in England. The dinner was much more American than any we had seen in Sweden. In the centre of the table was a high glass dish filled with a muskmelon & surrounded with flowers. The remainder of the dessert was not placed upon the table, but came on after meat, &c., as in our country. After soup, fish & meat, we had a nice baked apple pudding; & after this, the cloth was removed from the nicely polished round table, & the dessert of cake, apples, pears, preserves, nuts & raisins was placed upon it. Captain Condry from Newburyport dined there, a very pleasant and gentlemanly man. Mrs. Wijk urged us to remain to tea, but we left them soon after dinner.

Monday. 7. In the aft' walked around Gothenburg, a pleasant town, & much preferable as an abiding place to Stockholm, in my opinion. On returning home found Mr. and Mrs. Wijk. She looked sweetly & was dressed elegantly. They called to invite us to pass the morrow with them, at their country seat.-- Tuesday. 8. At eleven in the morning, took a carriage to Mr. Wijk's. A long & tedious ride, one & a quarter Swedish mile from town. We arrived there at one, found Mr. W[ijk] & his lady waiting to receive us. We took a walk round the grounds before dinner. The house built in a very pretty style & the grounds something like an English Park. An English gentleman, a brother-in-law of Mr. Wijk's dined with us. He has a country seat adjoining. After dinner, we walked to this gentleman's grounds. They are quite delighted with a fine lake near the house. We then visited the factories, which the owner, a man of great mechanical genius, has erected upon his grounds. We saw all the different stages the flax went through before weaving & lastly the weaving itself. We returned home & took tea with Mrs. Wijk & then bade adieu. Found on our return home Mr. Appleton had arrived from Stockholm. He goes to Copenhagen with us.

Wednesday. 9. At two in the aft' we left Gothenburg, in a little boat for the steamer station, which is three miles from the town. Mr. Wijk accompanied us to the wharf. When we arrived at the steamer pier--found the boat had not arrived from Christiana, & there we waited three hours for it. We left about 6 in the evening. The steamer crowded. We were obliged to sleep in the gentleman's cabin, & the cabin was entirely filled with hammocks swung one above another.--Thursday. 10. Arrived in Copenhagen at 2 P.M. Found good accommodations at the Hotel Royal. Monday. 14. Mr. Appleton & Mary G---- left us, for London. Tuesday. 15. In the morning went over the new palace, not yet entirely completed. It is a fine building, the rooms very neat, most of them carpeted. The carpet English, & upon the king's apartments of the most ordinary & coarsest Kidderminster. The Queen's were Brussels, but nothing extraordinary. In one large room was the king's throne--A gilded chair covered with crimson velvet, & his initials worked in gold upon it. The platform, & the steps by which you ascend to it, were also covered with crimson velvet. The window-curtains were superb--of crimson velvet & a gold vine wrought upon the edge of them. The Queen's apartments were more splendid than the king's. She had also a room similar to the king's, with a throne like his & curtains the same. The dancing hall was very fine with seven immense chandeliers in it.--The king and Queen both had their dining halls. There was a most splendid hall for dubbing knights. An immense room, with gallery all around it, supported by pillars which appeared like white marble, but were of some composition. The ceiling was very beautiful, white with raised gilt figures. The chapel was very fine; also the hall of justice, where criminals for high treason, I think, are tried. There is a throne of crimson velvet at one end, & three silver lions, with golden manes, as large as life & in very fierce attitudes are guarding it.

Thursday. 17. In the morning at the museum of "Northern Antiquities." The collection has been made since 20 years & is the largest in Europe. We were first shown the knives, chisels, arrows, &c., used before any metal was discovered & many--many years before Christianity. They were all of stone. We also saw the first rude urns which were used for the burial of dead bodies. Gold, silver & copper were discovered before iron; when iron was discovered it was for a long time so valuable, that we saw that instruments were made of copper & only pointed with iron. Thus we were shown these instruments from their first rude state till they arrived quite at perfection. We also saw the gold rings & bracelets which the ancients wore, & which they cut off, piece by piece, to give in exchange for clothing or food before the use of money. We saw a beautiful ebony altar piece with gold & silver figures raised upon it. It was intended for a chapel of one of the former kings; but he afterwards altered his plan & erected a large church,--so that it has never been used.

I fear, my dear Aunt, you will find this all very stupid & tedious, & will not thank me much for the copious extracts from my poor little journal. I flatter myself, however, you will take an interest in all that we do & see, so I give you the best descriptions in my power. Copenhagen appears like a different place to us, from what it did when here before. Henry would like to pass the winter here, he is now so charmed with it. We have a much pleasanter situation, than when here before, & coming from Sweden any place would be quite delightful. Indeed it seems now quite like London--the cries remind us of that city & it appears almost as noisy. How different from our first impression of Copenhagen! but then we were direct from London & after that immense and overpowering place everything seems dull and lifeless. We shall probably leave here this week Thursday, & shall take these letters to Hamburg with us, with the hopes of sending them directly to America from there. Henry sends books to the college from here, but it is so uncertain when they go I do not like to leave my letters. How lonely you will be without Sammy this winter; I feel very glad he has entered as Freshman, for we shall have him a year longer with us. Give much love to all from us--Clara is very well and seems very happy. She enjoys travelling very much, & is just as good & excellent a girl as ever--Henry desires very much love to Aunt Lucia--accept much from your ever affectionate

MARY.

To MISS LUCIA WADSWORTH, Portland, Me.

{30 Life, i. 205; also Harvard College Papers [MS.], vi. 290.}

{31 Harvard College Papers, 2d ser. vii. 1.}

{32 Harvard College Papers, 2d ser. vii. 10.}

{33 The journal is missing from the MS., having doubtless been retained by the father. A long extract from it will be found in the Life, i. 216.}

CHAPTER IX

ILLNESS AND DEATH OF MRS. LONGFELLOW

This series of happy travelling narratives was suddenly interrupted by the following letters, now first printed, to the father of the young wife.

ROTTERDAM, Dec. 1, 1835.

MY DEAR SIR,--I trust that my last letter to my father has in some measure prepared your mind for the melancholy intelligence which this will bring to you. Our beloved Mary is no more. She expired on Sunday morning, Nov. 29, without pain or suffering, either of body or mind, and with entire resignation to the will of her heavenly Father. Though her sickness was long, yet I could not bring myself to think it dangerous until near its close. Indeed, I did not abandon all hope of her recovery till within a very few hours of her dissolution, and to me the blow was so sudden, that I have hardly yet recovered energy enough to write you the particulars of this solemn and mournful event. When I think, however, upon the goodness and purity of her life, and the holy and peaceful death she died, I feel great consolation in my bereavement, and can say, "Father, thy will be done."

Knowing the delicate state of Mary's health, I came all the way from Stockholm with fear and trembling, and with the exception of one day's ride from Kiel to Hamburg we came the whole distance by water. Unfortunately our passage from Hamburg to Amsterdam in the Steamboat was rather rough, and Mary was quite unwell. On the night of our arrival the circumstance occurred to which I alluded in my last, [the premature birth of a child] and which has had this fatal termination.... In Amsterdam we remained three weeks; and Mary seemed to be quite restored and was anxious to be gone. To avoid a possibility of fatigue we took three days to come to this place--a distance of only forty miles; and on our arrival here Mary was in excellent spirits and to all appearances very well. But alas! the same night she had a relapse which caused extreme debility, with a low fever, and nervous headache. This was on the 23d October. In a day or two she was better, and on the 27th worse again. After this she seemed to recover slowly, and sat up for the first time on the 11th, though only for a short while. This continued for a day or two longer, till she felt well enough to sit up for nearly an hour. And then she was seized with a violent rheumatism, and again took to her bed from which she never more arose.

During all this she was very patient, and generally cheerful, tho' at times her courage fainted and she thought that she should not recover,--wishing only that she could see her friends at home once more before she died. At such moments she loved to repeat these lines [by Andrews Norton], which seemed to soothe her feelings:--

"Father! I thank thee! may no thought E'er deem thy chastisements severe. But may this heart, by sorrow taught, Calm each wild wish, each idle fear."

On Sunday, the 22nd, all her pain had left her, and she said she had not felt so well during her sickness. On this day, too, we received a letter from Margaret, which gave her great pleasure, and renovated her spirits very much. But still from day to day she gained no strength. In this situation she continued during the whole week--perfectly calm, cheerful and without any pain. On Friday another letter came from Margaret, and she listened to it with greatest delight. A few minutes afterwards a letter from you and Eliza was brought in, which I reserved for the next day. When I went to her on Saturday morning I found her countenance much changed, and my heart sank within me. Till this moment I had indulged the most sanguine hopes;--but now my fears overmastered them. She was evidently worse, though she felt as well as usual. The day passed without change; and towards evening, as she seemed a little restless and could not sleep, I sat down by her bedside, and read your letter and Eliza's to her. O, I shall never forget how her eyes and her whole countenance brightened, and with what a heavenly smile she looked up into my face as I read. My own hopes revived again to see that look; but alas! this was the last gleam of the dying lamp. Towards ten o'clock she felt a slight oppression in the chest, with a difficulty of breathing. I sat down by her side and tried to cheer her; and as her respiration became more difficult, she said to me, "Why should I be troubled; If I die God will take me to himself." And from this moment she was perfectly calm, excepting for a single instant, when she exclaimed, "O, my dear Father; how he will mourn for me." A short time afterwards she thanked Clara for her kindness, and clasping her arms affectionately round my neck, kissed me, and said, "Dear Henry, do not forget me!" and after this, "Tell my dear friends at home that I thought of them at the last hour." I then read to her from the Church Litany the prayers for the sick and dying; and as the nurse spoke of sending for Dr. Bosworth, the Episcopal clergyman, Mary said she should like to see him, and I accordingly sent. He came about one o'clock, but at this time Mary became apparently insensible to what was around her; and at half-past one she ceased to breathe.

Thus all the hopes I had so fondly cherished of returning home with my dear Mary in happiness and renovated health have in the providence of God ended in disappointment and sorrow unspeakable. All that I have left to me in my affliction is the memory of her goodness, her gentleness, her affection for me--unchangeable in life and in death--and the hope of meeting her again hereafter, where there shall be no more sickness, nor sorrow, nor suffering, nor death. I feel, too, that she must be infinitely, oh, infinitely happier now than when with us on earth, and I say to myself,--

"Peace! peace! she is not dead, she does not sleep! She has awakened from the dream of life."

With my most affectionate remembrance to Eliza and Margaret, and my warmest sympathies with you all, very truly yours,

HENRY W. LONGFELLOW.

On the 2d of December the young husband left Rotterdam for Heidelberg. There he spent the winter, like Paul Flemming of "Hyperion," and buried himself in "old dusty books." He met many men who interested him, Schlosser, Gervinus, and Mittermaier, and also Bryant, the poet, from his own country, whom he saw for the first time. An added sorrow came to him in the death of his brother-in-law and dearest friend, George W. Pierce, "He the young and strong," as he afterwards wrote in his "Footsteps of Angels;" but in accordance with the advice of his friend Ticknor he absorbed himself in intellectual labor, taking the direction of a careful study of German literature. This he traced from its foundations down to Jean Paul Richter, who was for him, as for many other Americans of the same period, its high-water mark, even to the exclusion of Goethe. It will be remembered that Longfellow's friend, Professor Felton, translated not long after, and very likely with Longfellow's aid or counsel, Menzel's "History of German Literature," in which Goethe is made quite a secondary figure.

It is also to be noticed that George Bancroft, one of the half dozen men in America who had studied at a German University, wrote about the same time a violent attack on Goethe in the Boston "Christian Examiner," in which he pronounced him far inferior to Voltaire, "not in genius and industry only, but still more in morality." He says of him farther, "He imitates, he reproduces, he does not create and he does not build up.... His chances at popularity are diminishing. Twaddle will not pass long for wisdom. The active spirit of movement and progress finds in his works little that attracts sympathy."{34} It is to be remembered in the same connection that Longfellow, in 1837, wrote to his friend, George W. Greene, of "Jean Paul Richter, the most magnificent of the German prose writers,"{35} and it was chiefly on Richter that his prose style was formed.

In June he left Heidelberg for the Tyrol and Switzerland, where the scene of "Hyperion" was laid. He called it "quite a sad and lonely journey," but it afterwards led to results both in his personal and literary career. He sailed for home in October and established himself in Cambridge in December, 1836. The following letter to his wife's sister was written after his return.

CAMBRIDGE, Sunday evening.

MY DEAR ELIZA,--By tomorrow's steamboat I shall send you two trunks, containing the clothes which once belonged to your sister. What I have suffered in getting them ready to send to you, I cannot describe. It is not necessary, that I should. Cheerful as I may have seemed to you at times, there are other times, when it seems to me that my heart would break. The world considers grief unmanly, and is suspicious of that sorrow, which is expressed by words and outward signs. Hence we strive to be gay and put a cheerful courage on, when our souls are very sad. But there are hours, when the world is shut out, and we can no longer hear the voices, that cheer and encourage us. To me such hours come daily. I was so happy with my dear Mary, that it is very hard to be alone. The sympathies of friendship are doubtless something--but after all how little, how unsatisfying they are to one who has been so loved as I have been! This is a selfish sorrow, I know: but neither reason nor reflection can still it. Affliction makes us childish. A grieved and wounded heart is hard to be persuaded. We do not wish to have our sorrow lessened. There are wounds, which are never entirely healed. A thousand associations call up the past, with all its gloom and shadow. Often a mere look or sound--a voice--the odor of a flower--the merest trifle is enough to awaken within me deep and unutterable emotions. Hardly a day passes, that some face, or familiar object, or some passage in the book I am reading does not call up the image of my beloved wife so vividly, that I pause and burst into tears,--and sometimes cannot rally again for hours.

And yet, my dear Eliza, in a few days, and we shall all be gone, and others sorrowing and rejoicing as we now do, will have taken our places: and we shall say, how childish it was for us to mourn for things so transitory. There may be some consolation in this; but we are nevertheless children. Our feelings overcome us.

Farewell. Give my kind regards to all, and believe me most truly and affectionately, your friend,

HENRY W. LONGFELLOW.{36}

{34 Christian Examiner, July, 1839, xxvi. 363-367.}

{35 Life, i. 259.}

{36 MS. letter.}

CHAPTER X

CRAIGIE HOUSE

In entering on the duties of his Harvard professorship (December, 1836) Longfellow took rooms at the Craigie House in Cambridge. This house, so long his residence, has been claimed as having more historic interest than any house in New England, both from the fact of his ownership and of its having been the headquarters of General Washington during the siege of Boston. It has even been called from these two circumstances the best known residence in the United States, with the exception of Mt. Vernon, with which it has some analogy both in position and in aspect. It overlooks the Charles River as the other overlooks the Potomac, though the latter view is of course far more imposing, and the Craigie House wants the picturesque semicircle of outbuildings so characteristic of Mt. Vernon, while it is far finer in respect to rooms, especially in the upper stories. It was built, in all probability, in 1759 by Colonel John Vassall, whose family owned the still older house across the way now called the Batchelder House; and there is a tradition of a subterranean passage between the two houses, although this has hitherto been sought in vain. Both these dwellings belonged to a series of large houses on Brattle Street, called Tory Row, whose proprietors were almost all kinsfolk, owned West India estates and slaves, entertained company in great affluence, according to the descriptions of the Baroness Riedesel, and were almost all forced to leave the country at the approach of the Revolution. Tradition recalls a Twelfth Night party given by Mrs. Washington in 1776, she having come to visit her husband during his residence in Cambridge. "She arrived in great ceremony, with a coach and four black horses, with postilions and servants in scarlet livery. During her visit she and her husband celebrated their wedding anniversary, though the General had to be much persuaded by his aides."{37} The southeastern room, afterwards Longfellow's study, had been Washington's office, and the chamber above it his private room, this being Longfellow's original study. The house was bought about 1792, the dates being a little uncertain, by Andrew Craigie, apothecary-general of the northern department of the Revolutionary army, who made additions to the house, which was described as a princely establishment.{38} Mr. Craigie sometimes entertained a hundred guests at the Commencement festival, and had among his other guests the celebrated Talleyrand and the Duke of Kent, Queen Victoria's father, then Prince Edward. Mr. Craigie had large business transactions, speculated extensively but at last unsuccessfully in real estate, and died in 1819. His wife long outlived him, and being poor, let rooms to various inmates. Edward Everett took his bride there in 1822, and so did

President Jared Sparks in 1832. Five years after, Longfellow took the rooms, and thus describes his first visit to Mrs. Craigie:--

"The first time I was in Craigie House was on a beautiful afternoon in the year 1837. I came to see Mr. McLane, a law-student, who occupied the southeastern chamber. The window-blinds were closed, but through them came a pleasant breeze, and I could see the waters of the Charles gleaming in the meadows. McLane left Cambridge in August, and I took possession of his room, making use of it as a library or study, and having the adjoining chamber for my bedroom. At first Mrs. Craigie declined to let me have rooms. I remember how she looked as she stood, in her white turban, with her hands crossed behind her, snapping her gray eyes. She had resolved, she said, to take no more students into the house. But her manner changed when I told her who I was. She said that she had read 'Outre-Mer,' of which one number was lying on her side-board. She then took me all over the house and showed me every room in it, saying, as we went into each, that I could not have that one. She finally consented to my taking the rooms mentioned above, on condition that the door leading into the back entry should be locked on the outside. Young Habersham, of Savannah, a friend of Mrs. Craigie's, occupied at that time the other front chamber. He was a skilful performer on the flute. Like other piping birds, he took wing for the rice-fields of the South when the cold weather came, and I remained alone with the widow in her castle. The back part of the house was occupied, however, by her farmer. His wife supplied my meals and took care of my rooms. She was a giantess, and very pious in words; and when she brought in my breakfast frequently stopped to exhort me. The exorbitant rate at which she charged my board was rather at variance with her preaching. Her name was Miriam; and Felton called her 'Miriam, the profitess.' Her husband was a meek little man.

"The winter was a rather solitary one, and the house very still. I used to hear Mrs. Craigie go down to breakfast at nine or ten in the morning and go up to bed at eleven at night. During the day she seldom left the parlor, where she sat reading the newspapers and the magazines,--occasionally a volume of Voltaire. She read also the English Annuals, of which she had a large collection. Occasionally, the sound of voices announced a visitor; and she sometimes enlivened the long evenings with a half-forgotten tune upon an old piano-forte.

"During the following summer the fine old elms in front of the house were attacked by canker-worms, which, after having devoured the leaves, came spinning down in myriads. Mrs. Craigie used to sit by the open windows and let them crawl over her white turban unmolested. She would have nothing done to protect the trees from these worms; she used to say, 'Why, sir, they are our fellow-worms; they have as good a right to live as we have.'"

It was certainly a strange chance which threw the young poet, on his return from Europe, into the curiously cosmopolitan atmosphere of Mrs. Craigie's mind. The sale catalogue of her books lies before me, a mass of perhaps five hundred odd volumes of worthy or worthless literature: Goethe's "Werther" beside the American "Frugal Housewife," and Heath's "Book of Beauty" beside "Hannah More." Yet it was doubtless the only house in Cambridge which then held complete sets of Voltaire and Diderot, of Moliere. Some of the books thus sold form a part to this day of the Longfellow library at Craigie House; but there is no reference to the poet in the original catalogue, except that it includes "Outre-Mer," No. 1, doubtless the same copy which he saw lying on the sideboard.

Mr. J. E. Worcester, the lexicographer, shared the house with Longfellow, as did for a time Miss Sally Lowell, an aunt of the poet. Mr. Worcester bought it for himself, and ultimately sold it to Mr. Nathan Appleton, father of the second Mrs. Longfellow, to whom he presented it. Part of the ten magnificent elms of which Longfellow wrote in 1839 have disappeared. The ground has been improved by the low-fenced terrace which he added, and the grounds opposite, given by the poet's children to the Longfellow Memorial Association, have been graded into a small public park descending nearly to the river. Within the house all remains much the same, Longfellow's library never having been scattered, although his manuscripts and proof-sheets, which he preserved and caused to be bound in their successive stages in the most orderly manner, have now been transferred to a fire-proof building for greater security. The "old clock on the stairs," which he himself placed there, still ticks and strikes the hour; and one can see cracks in the stairway through which the mysterious letters dropped morning after morning, as told in the story of "Esther Wynne's Love Letters," by the accomplished author known as Saxe Holm. The actual letters were more commonplace, but they were apparently written by a schoolgirl under Mr. Craigie's care; and there was a tradition, not very well authenticated, that Longfellow himself had planned to make them the subject of a poem before Saxe Holm or Helen Hunt--as the case may be--had anticipated him in prose.

Such was the house where Longfellow resided for the rest of his life; seven years of which passed before his second wedded life began. The following letter, taken from the Harvard College papers, will show the interest he took in the estate.

MY DEAR SIR [President Quincy],--Will you have the goodness to lay before the Corporation, at their next meeting, my request concerning the trees, which I mentioned to you the last time I had the pleasure of seeing you; viz. that they would permit me to take from the College grounds 3 elm trees to be placed in front of the Craigie House.

I am endeavoring to replace, as well as possible, the old elms, and find it difficult to obtain many of the size I desire. Some parts of the College ground are so thickly planted that a tree may be removed, here & there, without at all impairing the beauty of the grounds. I therefore request permission to remove any 3 trees that the College Steward shall say may be taken without detriment to the College property.

Yrs very truly,

HENRY W. LONGFELLOW.

CAMBRIDGE, Dec. 29 [1843].{39}

{37 Miss Alice M. Longfellow in The Cambridge Tribune, April 21, 1900, page 4.}

{38 A history of this house from original documents was prepared by Samuel S. Green, of Worcester, and was read by him before the American Antiquarian Society, April 25, 1900, and published in their documents.}

{39 Harvard College Papers [MS.], 2d ser. xii. 26.}

CHAPTER XI

"Outre-Mer" had been published some time before, with moderate success, but "Hyperion" was destined to attract far more attention. It is first mentioned in his journal on September 13, 1838, though in a way which shows that it had been for some time in preparation, and its gradual development is traceable through the same channel. One entire book, for instance, was written and suppressed, namely, "St. Clair's Day Book," the hero having first been christened Hyperion, then St. Clair, and then Paul Flemming. Its author wrote of it, "I called it 'Hyperion,' because it moves on high among clouds and stars, and expresses the various aspirations of the soul of man. It is all modelled on this idea, style and all. It contains my cherished thoughts for three years."{40}

The cordiality with which "Hyperion" was received was due partly to the love story supposed to be implied in it, and largely to the new atmosphere of German life and literature which it opened to Americans. It must always be remembered that the kingdom in which Germany then ruled was not then, as now, a kingdom of material force and business enterprise, but as Germans themselves claimed, a kingdom of the air; and into that realm Hyperion gave to Americans the first glimpse. The faults and limitations which we now see in it were then passed by, or visible only to such keen critics as Orestes A. Brownson, who wrote thus of it in "The Boston Quarterly Review," then the ablest of American periodicals except "The Dial:" "I do not like the book. It is such a journal as a man who reads a great deal makes from the scraps in his table-drawer. Yet it has not the sincerity or quiet touches which give interest to the real journals of very common persons. It is overloaded with prettinesses, many of which would tell well in conversation, but being rather strown over than woven into his narrative, deform where they should adorn. You cannot guess why the book was written, unless because the author were tired of reading these morceaux to himself, for there has been no fusion or fermentation to bring on the hour of utterance. Then to me the direct personal relation in which we are brought to the author is unpleasing. Had he but idealized his tale, or put on the veil of poetry! But as it is, we are embarrassed by his extreme communicativeness, and wonder that a man, who seems in other respects to have a mind of delicate texture, could write a letter about his private life to a public on which he had as yet established no claim.... Indeed this book will not add to the reputation of its author, which stood so fair before its publication."{41} This is the criticism of which Longfellow placidly wrote, "I understand there is a spicy article against me in the 'Boston Quarterly.' I shall get it as soon as I can; for, strange as you may think it, these things give me no pain."{42}

Mr. Howells, in one of the most ardent eulogies ever written upon the works of Longfellow, bases his admiration largely upon the claim "that his art never betrays the crudeness or imperfection of essay,"--that is, of experiment.{43} It would be interesting to know whether this accomplished author, looking back upon "Hyperion" more than thirty years later, could reindorse this strong assertion. To others, I fancy, however attractive and even fascinating the book may still remain, it has about it a distinctly youthful quality which, while sometimes characterizing even his poetry, unquestionably marked his early prose. A later and younger critic says more truly of it, I think, "Plainly in the style of Richter, with all the mingled grandeur and grotesqueness of the German romanticists, it is scarcely now a favorite with the adult reader; though the young, obedient to some vague embryonic law, still find in it for a season the pleasure, the thrilling melancholy, which their grandfathers found."{44} But Professor Carpenter, speaking from the point of view of the younger generation, does not fail to recognize that Paul Flemming's complaints cease when he reads the tombstone inscription which becomes the motto of the book; and I recall with pleasure that, being a youth nurtured on "Hyperion," I selected that passage for the text of my boyish autobiography written in the Harvard "Class Book" at the juvenile age of seventeen. Dozens of youths were perhaps adopting the motto in the same way at the same time, and it is useless to deny to a book which thus reached youthful hearts the credit of having influenced the whole period of its popularity.

Apart from the personal romance which his readers attached to it, the book had great value as the first real importation into our literature of the wealth of German romance and song. So faithful and ample are its local descriptions that a cheap edition of it is always on sale at Heidelberg, and every English and American visitor to that picturesque old city seems to know the book by heart. Bearing it in his hand, the traveller still climbs the rent summit of the Gesprengte Thurm and looks down upon the throng in the castle gardens; or inquires vainly for the ruined linden-tree, or gives a sigh to the fate of Emma of Ilmenau, and murmurs solemnly,--as a fat and red-faced Englishman once murmured to me on that storied spot,--"That night there fell a star from heaven!" There is no doubt that under the sway of the simpler style now prevailing, much of the rhetoric of "Hyperion" seems turgid, some of its learning obtrusive, and a good deal of its emotion forced; but it was nevertheless an epoch-making book for a generation of youths and maidens, and it still retains its charm. The curious fact, however, remains--a fact not hitherto noticed, I think, by biographers or critics--that at the very time when the author was at work on "Hyperion," there was a constant reaction in his mind that was carrying him in the direction of more strictly American subjects, handled under a simpler treatment. He wrote on September 13, 1838, "Looked over my notes and papers for 'Hyperion.' Long for leisure to begin once more." It is impossible to say how long a preparation this implies; it may have been months or years. Yet the following letter to a young girl, his wife's youngest sister, shows how, within less than a year previous, his observation had been again turned towards the American Indians as a theme.

CAMBRIDGE, October 29, 1837.

MY DEAR MARGARET,--I was very much delighted with your present of the slippers. They are too pretty to be trodden under foot; yet such is their destiny, and shall be accomplished, as soon as may be. The colors look beautifully upon the drab ground; much more so than on the black. Don't you think so? I should have answered your note, and sent you my thanks, by Alexander on Wednesday last; but when I last saw him, I had not received the package. Therefore you must not imagine from my delay, that I do not sufficiently appreciate the gift....

There is nothing very new in Boston, which after all is a gossiping kind of Little Peddlington, if you know what that is; if you don't, you must read the story. People take too much cognizance of their neighbors; interest themselves too much in what no way concerns them. However, it is no great matter.

There are Indians here: savage fellows;--one Black-Hawk and his friends, with naked shoulders and red blankets wrapped about their bodies:--the rest all grease and Spanish brown and vermillion. One carries a great war-club, and wears horns on his head; another had his face painted like a grid-iron, all in bands:--another is all red, like a lobster; and another black and blue, in great daubs of paint laid on not sparingly. Queer fellows!--One great champion of the Fox nation had a short pipe in his mouth, smoking with great self-complacency as he marched out of the City Hall: another was smoking a cigar! Withal, they looked very formidable. Hard customers....

Very truly yours

H. W. L.{45}

Note, again, how this tendency to home themes asserts itself explicitly in Longfellow's notice of Hawthorne's "Twice-Told Tales" at about the same time in "The North American Review," (July, 1837):--

"One of the most prominent characteristics of these tales is, that they are national in their character. The author has wisely chosen his themes among the traditions of New England; the dusty legends of 'the good Old Colony times, when we lived under a king.' This is the right material for story. It seems as natural to make tales out of old tumble-down traditions, as canes and snuff-boxes out of old steeples, or trees planted by great men. The puritanical times begin to look romantic in the distance. Who would not like to have strolled through the city of Agamenticus, where a market was held every week, on Wednesday, and there were two annual fairs at St. James's and St. Paul's? Who would not like to have been present at the court of the Worshipful Thomas Gorges, in those palmy days of the law, when Tom Heard was fined five shillings for being drunk, and John Payne the same, 'for swearing one oath'? Who would not like to have seen the time, when Thomas Taylor was presented to the grand jury 'for abusing Captain Raynes, being in authority, by thee-ing and thou-ing him;' and John Wardell likewise, for denying Cambridge College to be an ordinance of God; and when some were fined for winking at comely damsels in church; and others for being common-sleepers there on the Lord's day? Truly, many quaint and quiet customs, many comic scenes and strange adventures, many wild and wondrous things, fit for humorous tale, and soft, pathetic story, lie all about us here in New England. There is no tradition of the Rhine nor of the Black Forest, which can compare in beauty with that of the Phantom Ship. The Flying Dutchman of the Cape, and the Klabotermann of the Baltic, are nowise superior. The story of Peter Rugg, the man who could not find Boston, is as good as that told by Gervase of Tilbury, of a man who gave himself to the devils by an unfortunate imprecation, and was used by them as a wheelbarrow; and the Great Carbuncle of the White Mountains shines with no less splendor, than that which illuminated the subterranean palace in Rome, as related by William of Malmesbury. Truly, from such a Fortunatus's pocket and wishing-cap, a tale-bearer may furnish forth a sufficiency of 'peryllous adventures right espouventables, bryfefly compyled and pyteous for to here.'"

We must always remember that Longfellow came forward at a time when cultivated Americans were wasting a great deal of superfluous sympathy on themselves. It was the general impression that the soil was barren, that the past offered no material and they must be European or die. Yet Longfellow's few predecessors had already made themselves heard by disregarding this tradition and taking what they found on the spot. Charles Brockden Brown, although his style was exotic and Godwinish, yet found his themes among American Indians and in the scenes of the yellow fever in Philadelphia. It was not Irving who invested the Hudson with romance, but the Hudson that inspired Irving. When in 1786, Mrs. Josiah Quincy, then a young girl, sailed upon that river in a sloop, she wrote, "Our captain had a legend for every scene, either supernatural or traditional or of actual occurrence during the war, and not a mountain reared its head unconnected with some marvellous story." Irving was then but three years old, yet Ichabod Crane and Rip Van Winkle or their prototypes were already on the spot waiting for biographers; and it was much the same with Cooper, who was not born until three years later. What was needed was self-confidence and a strong literary desire to take the materials at hand. Irving, Cooper, Dana, had already done this; but Longfellow followed with more varied gifts, more thorough training; the "Dial" writers followed in their turn, and a distinctive American literature was born, this quality reaching a climax in Thoreau, who frankly wrote, "I have travelled a great deal--in Concord."

And while thus Longfellow found his desire for a national literature strengthened at every point by the example of his classmate Hawthorne, so he may have learned much, though not immediately, through the warning unconsciously given by Bryant, against the perils of undue moralizing. Bryant's early poem, "To a Water-Fowl," was as profound in feeling and as perfect in structure as anything of Longfellow's, up to the last verse, which some profane critic compared to a tin kettle of moralizing, tied to the legs of the flying bird. Whittier's poems had almost always some such appendage, and he used to regret in later life that he had not earlier been contented to leave his moral for the reader to draw, or in other words, to lop off habitually the last verse of each poem. Apart from this there was a marked superiority, even on the didactic side, in Longfellow's moralizing as compared with Bryant's. There is no light or joy in the "Thanatopsis;" but Longfellow, like Whittier, was always hopeful. It was not alone that he preached, as an eminent British critic once said to me, "a safe piety," but his religious impulse was serene and even joyous, and this under the pressure of the deepest personal sorrows.

It is also to be observed that Longfellow wrote in this same number of "The North American Review" (July, 1837) another paper which was prophetic with regard to prose style, as was the Hawthorne essay in respect to thought. It was a review of Tegner's "Frithiof's Saga" which showed a power of description, brought to bear on Swedish life and scenery, which he really never quite attained in "Hyperion," because it was there sometimes vitiated by a slightly false note. A portion of it was used afterwards as a preface to his second volume of poems ("Ballads and Other Poems"), a preface regarded by some good critics as Longfellow's best piece of prose work. It was, at any rate, impossible not to recognize a fresh and vigorous quality in a descriptive passage opening thus; and I can myself testify that it stamped itself on the memories of young readers almost as vividly as the ballads which followed:--

"There is something patriarchal still lingering about rural life in Sweden, which renders it a fit theme for song. Almost primeval simplicity reigns over that northern land,--almost primeval solitude and stillness. You pass out from the gate of the city, and, as if by magic, the scene changes to a wild, woodland landscape. Around you are forests of fir. Overhead hang the long, fan-like branches, trailing with moss, and heavy with red and blue cones. Under foot is a carpet of yellow leaves; and the air is warm and balmy. On a wooden bridge you cross a little silver stream; and anon come forth into a pleasant and sunny land of farms. Wooden fences divide the adjoining fields. Across the road are gates, which are opened by troops of children. The peasants take off their hats as you pass; you sneeze, and they cry, 'God bless you.' The houses in the villages and smaller towns are all built of hewn timber, and for the most part painted red. The floors of the taverns are strewn with the fragrant tips of fir boughs. In many villages there are no taverns, and the peasants take turns in receiving travellers. The thrifty housewife shows you into the best chamber, the walls of which are hung round with rude pictures from the Bible; and brings you her heavy silver spoons,--an heirloom,--to dip the curdled milk from the pan. You have oaten cakes baked some months before; or bread with anise-seed and coriander in it, or perhaps a little pine bark."

{40 Life, i. 353.}

{41 Boston Quarterly Review, January, 1840, iii. 128.}

{42 Life, i. 354.}

{43 North American Review, civ. 537.}

{44 Carpenter's Longfellow, p. 55.}

{45 MS.}

CHAPTER XII

VOICES OF THE NIGHT

There was never any want of promptness or of industry about Longfellow, though his time was apt to be at the mercy of friends or strangers. "Hyperion" appeared in the summer of 1839, and on September 12, 1839, he writes the title of his volume, "Voices of the Night;" five days later he writes, still referring to it:--

"First, I shall publish a collection of poems. Then,--History of English Poetry.

"Studies in the Manner of Claude Lorraine; a series of Sketches.

"Count Cagliostro; a novel.

"The Saga of Hakon Jarl; a poem."

It is to be noticed that neither of these four projects, except it be the second, seems to imply that national character of which he dreamed when the paper in "The North American Review" was written. It is also to be noticed that, as often happens with early plans of authors, none of these works ever appeared, and perhaps not even the beginning was made. The title of "The Saga" shows that his mind was still engaged with Norse subjects. Two months after he writes, "Meditating what I shall write next. Shall it be two volumes more of 'Hyperion;' or a drama of Cotton Mather?" Here we come again upon American ground, yet he soon quits it. He adds after an interruption, "Cotton Mather? or a drama on the old poetic legend of Der Armer Heinrich? The tale is exquisite. I have a heroine as sweet as Imogen, could I but paint her so. I think I must try this." Here we have indicated the theme of the "Golden Legend." Meantime he was having constant impulses to write special poems, which he often mentioned as Psalms. One of these was the "Midnight Mass for the Dying Year," which he first called an "Autumnal Chant." Soon after he says, "Wrote a new Psalm of Life. It is 'The Village Blacksmith.'" It is to be noticed that the "Prelude," probably written but a short time before the publication of "Voices of the Night," includes those allusions which called forth the criticism of Margaret Fuller to the "Pentecost" and the "bishop's caps." Yet after all, the American Jews still observe Whitsunday under the name of Pentecost, and the flower mentioned may be the Mitella diphylla, a strictly North American species, though without any distinctly "golden ring." It has a faint pink suffusion, while the presence of a more marked golden ring in a similar and commoner plant, the Tiarella Pennsylvanica, leads one to a little uncertainty as to which flower was meant, a kind of doubt which would never accompany a floral description by Tennyson.

It is interesting to put beside this inspirational aspect of poetry the fact that the poet at one time planned a newspaper with his friends Felton and Cleveland, involving such a perfectly practical and business-like communication as this, with his publisher, Samuel Colman, which is as follows:{46}--

CAMBRIDGE, July 6, 1839.

MY DEAR SIR,--In compliance with your wishes I have ordered 2200 copies of Hyperion to be printed. I do it with the understanding, that you will give your notes for $250 each, instead of the sums mentioned in the agreement: and that I shall be allowed 50 copies instead of 25 for distribution. This will leave you 150, which strikes me as a very large number.

The first Vol. (212 pp.) will be done to-day: and the whole in a fortnight, I hope. It is very handsome; and those who praise you for publishing handsome books, will have some reason for saying so.

Will you have the books, or any part of them done up here?--and in the English style, uncut?--Those for the Boston market I should think you would.

With best regards to Mellen and Cutler,

Very truly yours in haste

LONGFELLOW.

P. S. By the way; I was shocked yesterday to see in the New York Review that Undine was coming out in your Library of Romance. This is one of the tales of the Wonderhorn. Have you forgotten? I intend to come to New York, as soon as I get through with printing Hyperion; and we will bring this design to an arrangement, and one more beside.

Addressed to SAMUEL COLMAN, ESQ. 8 Astor House, New York.

That was at a time when it was quite needful that American authors should be business-like, since American publishers sometimes were not. The very man to whom this letter was addressed became bankrupt six months later; half the edition of "Hyperion" (1200 copies) was seized by creditors and was locked up, so that the book was out of the market for four months. "No matter," the young author writes in his diary, "I had the glorious satisfaction of writing it." Meanwhile the "Knickerbocker" had not paid its contributors for three years, and the success of "Voices of the Night" was regarded as signal, because the publisher had sold 850 copies in three weeks.

The popularity of the "Voices of the Night," though not universal, was very great. Hawthorne wrote to him of these poems, "Nothing equal to some of them was ever written in this world,--this western world, I mean; and it would not hurt my conscience much to include the other hemisphere."{47} Halleck also said of the "Skeleton in Armor" that there was "nothing like it in the language," and Poe wrote to Longfellow, May 3, 1841, "I cannot refrain from availing myself of this, the only opportunity I may ever have, to assure the author of the 'Hymn to the Night,' of the 'Beleaguered City,' and of the 'Skeleton in Armor' of the fervent admiration with which his genius has inspired me."

In most of the criticisms of Longfellow's earlier poetry, including in this grouping even the "Psalm of Life," we lose sight of that fine remark of Sara Coleridge, daughter of the poet, who said to Aubrey de Vere, "However inferior the bulk of a young man's poetry may be to that of the poet when mature, it generally possesses some passages with a special freshness of their own and an inexplicable charm to be found in them alone." Professor Wendell's criticisms on Longfellow, in many respects admirable, do not seem to me quite to recognize this truth, nor yet the companion fact that while Poe took captive the cultivated but morbid taste of the French public, it was Longfellow who called forth more translators in all nations than all other Americans put together. If, as Professor Wendell thinks, the foundation of Longfellow's fame was the fact that he introduced our innocent American public to "the splendors of European civilization,"{48} how is it that his poems won and held such a popularity among those who already had these splendors at their door? It is also to be remembered that he was, if this were all, in some degree preceded by Bryant, who had opened the doors of Spanish romance to young Americans even before Longfellow led them to Germany and Italy.

Yet a common ground of criticism on Longfellow's early poems lay in the very simplicity which made them, then and ever since, so near to the popular heart. Digby, in one of his agreeable books, compares them in this respect to the paintings of Cuyp in these words: "The objects of Cuyp, for instance, are few in number and commonplace in their character--a bit of land and water, a few cattle and figures in no way remarkable. His power, says a critic, reminds me of some of the short poems of Longfellow, where things in themselves most prosaic are flooded with a kind of poetic light from the inner soul."{49} It is quite certain that one may go farther in looking back upon the development of our literature and can claim that this simplicity was the precise contribution needed at that early and formative period. Literature in a new country naturally tends to the florid, and one needs only to turn to the novels of Charles Brockden Brown, or even Bancroft's "History of the United States," to see how eminently this was the case in America. Whatever the genius of Poe, for instance, we can now see that he represented, in this respect, a dangerous tendency, and Poe's followers and admirers exemplified it in its most perilous form. Take, for instance, such an example as that of Dr. Thomas Holley Chivers of Georgia, author of "Eonchs of Ruby," a man of whom Bayard Taylor wrote in 1871, speaking of that period thirty years earlier, "that something wonderful would come out of Chivers."{50} It is certain that things wonderful came out of him at the very beginning, for we owe to him the statement that "as the irradiancy of a diamond depends upon its diaphanous translucency, so does the beauty of a poem upon its rhythmical crystallization of the Divine Idea." One cannot turn a page of Chivers without recognizing that he at his best was very closely allied to Poe at his worst. Such a verse as the following was not an imitation, but a twin blossom:--

"On the beryl-rimmed rebecs of Ruby Brought fresh from the hyaline streams, She played on the banks of the Yuba Such songs as she heard in her dreams, Like the heavens when the stars from their eyries Look down through the ebon night air, Where the groves by the Ouphantic Fairies Lit up for my Lily Adair, For my child-like Lily Adair, For my heaven-born Lily Adair, For my beautiful, dutiful Lily Adair."

It is easy to guess that Longfellow, in his "North American Review" article, drew from Dr. Chivers and his kin his picture of those "writers, turgid and extravagant," to be found in American literature. He farther says of them: "Instead of ideas, they give us merely the signs of ideas. They erect a great bridge of words, pompous and imposing, where there is hardly a drop of thought to trickle beneath. Is not he who thus apostrophizes the clouds, 'Ye posters of the wakeless air!' quite as extravagant as the Spanish poet, who calls a star a 'burning doubloon of the celestial bank'?"{51} It is a curious fact that this exuberant poet Chivers claimed a certain sympathy{52} with the Boston "Dial" and with the transcendental movement, which had a full supply of its own extravagances; and it is clear that between these two rhetorical extremes there was needed a voice for simplicity. Undoubtedly Bryant had an influence in the same direction of simplicity. But Bryant seemed at first curiously indifferent to Longfellow. "Voices of the Night" was published in 1839, and there appeared two years after, in 1841, a volume entitled "Selections from the American Poets," edited by Bryant, in which he gave eleven pages each to Percival and Carlos Wilcox, nine to Pierpont, eight to himself, and only four to Longfellow. It is impossible to interpret this proportion as showing that admiration which Bryant seems to have attributed to himself five years later when he wrote to him of the illustrated edition of his poems, "They appear to be more beautiful than on former readings, much as I then admired them. The exquisite music of your verse dwells more than ever on my ear."{53} Their personal relation remained always cordial, but never intimate, Longfellow always recognizing his early obligations to the elder bard and always keeping by him the first edition of Bryant's poems, published in 1821. Both poets were descended from a common pilgrim ancestry in John Alden and Priscilla Mullins, whose story Longfellow has told.{54}

Thus much for first experiences with the world of readers. The young professor's academical standing and services must be reserved for another chapter. But he at once found himself, apart from this, a member of a most agreeable social circle, for which his naturally cheerful temperament admirably fitted him. It is indeed doubtful if any Harvard professor of to-day could record in his note-books an equally continuous course of mild festivities. There are weeks when he never spends an evening at home. He often describes himself as "gloomy," but the gloom is never long visible. He constantly walks in and out of Boston, or drives to Brookline or Jamaica Plain; and whist and little suppers are never long omitted. Lowell was not as yet promoted to his friendship because of youth, nor had he and Holmes then been especially brought together, but Prescott, Sumner, Felton, and others constantly appear. He draws the line at a fancy ball, declining to costume himself for that purpose; and he writes that he never dances, but in other respects spends his evenings after his own inclination. Two years later, however, he mentions his purpose of going to a subscription ball "for the purpose of dancing with elderly ladies," who are, he thinks, "much more grateful for slight attentions than younger ones."

It is curious to find the fact made prominent by all contemporary critics, in their references to the young professor, that he was at this time not only neat in person, but with a standard of costume which made him rather exceptional. To those accustomed to the average dress of instructors in many colleges up to this day, this spirit of criticism may afford no surprise. His brother tells us that "good Mrs. Craigie thought he had somewhat too gay a look," and "had a fondness for colors in coats, waistcoats, and neckties." It will be remembered that in "Hyperion" he makes the Baron say to Paul Flemming, "The ladies already begin to call you Wilhelm Meister, and they say that your gloves are a shade too light for a strictly virtuous man." He wrote also to Sumner when in Europe: "If you have any tendency to curl your hair and wear gloves like Edgar in 'Lear,' do it before your return." It is a curious fact that he wrote of himself about the same time to his friend, George W. Greene, in Rome: "Most of the time am alone; smoke a good deal; wear a broad-brimmed hat, black frock coat, a black cane."{55}

Of the warmth of heart which lay beneath this perhaps worldly exterior, the following letter to his youthful sister-in-law gives evidence:--

Friday evening [1837].

MY GOOD, DEAR MADGE,--You do not know how sorry I am, that I cannot see you. But for a week past I have hardly left my chamber. I have been so ill as to give up all College duties, Lectures, &c.; and am very happy to get through--(as I trust I shall) without a fever, which I have been expecting for several days past. To-night I am better and have crawled off the sofa, to write you half a dozen lines.

My dear little child; I am truly delighted to know you are in Boston. It is an unexpected pleasure to me. Of course you mean to stay all summer; and I shall see you very often. Write me immediately; and tell me everything about everybody. I shall come and kiss you to death, as soon as my bodily strength will permit.

Till then very truly my little dear,

Yr. BROTHER HENRY.

{46 From the Chamberlain Collection of Autographs, Boston Public Library.}

{47 Life, i. 349.}

{48 Literary History of America, p. 384.}

{49 The Lovers Seat, London, i. 36.}

{50 Passages from the Correspondence of Rufus W. Griswold, p. 46.}

{51 North American Review, xxxiv. 75.}

{52 Passages from the Correspondence of Rufus W. Griswold, p. 46.}

{53 Life, ii. 31.}

{54 Bigelow's Life of Bryant, p. 3.}

{55 Life, i. 256, 304.}

CHAPTER XIII

THIRD VISIT TO EUROPE

The year 1841 was on the whole a rather dazzling period for the young poet. His first volume had been received with enthusiasm. His second volume was under way. He had a circle of friends always ready to criticise any new poem or to propose themes for other works; chief among the latter being his friend Samuel Ward, in New York, who suggested the "Phantom Ship," on the basis of a legend in Mather's "Magnalia," and urged the translation of Uhland's "Das Gl 點 k von Edenhall" and Pfizer's "Junggesell." A scrap of newspaper, bearing the seal of the State of New York with the motto "Excelsior," suggested the poem of that name. "The Skeleton in Armor" was included within the book and was originally to have given the title to it. Prescott, the historian, said that this poem and the "Hesperus" were the best imaginative poems since Coleridge's "Ancient Mariner." Reading the tenth chapter of Mark in Greek, Longfellow thought of "Blind Bartimeus." He wrote to his father that he liked the last two poems in the volume best, and thought them perhaps as good as anything he had written,--these being "Maidenhood" and "Excelsior." It was also in this year that he conceived the plan of the "Spanish Student" and of "a long and elaborate poem by the holy name of 'Christ,' the theme of which would be the various aspects of Christendom in the Apostolic, Middle, and Modern Ages." It shows the quiet persistence of the poet's nature that this plan, thus conceived in 1841, was brought to a final conclusion, more than thirty years after, in 1873, and under the very name originally conceived, that of "Christus." Thus much for this year of poetic achievement. His journals, as published by his brother, show the activity of social life which the year also included; and, above all, his regular academic work was of itself continuous and exhausting. In the schedule of university lectures, announced in the college catalogue for 1841-2, one finds the following entry: "On the French, Spanish, Italian, and German languages and literature, by Professor Longfellow." In the list of officers there appear only three instructors as doing the detailed work of instruction under this professor, and the lecturing was done entirely by him, occupying three hours a week, on the afternoons of Monday, Wednesday, and Friday. He was designated in the catalogue as "Smith Professor of the French and Spanish languages and literature and Professor of Belles Lettres," whatever this last phrase may have been construed as including. He had also the supervision of his subordinates, the examination of written exercises, and the attendance upon faculty meetings; and it certainly is no cause for wonder that the following letters should have passed between him and the college authorities.

[1839].

GENTLEMEN,--I respectfully beg leave to call your attention once more to the subject of my duties as Smith Professor in the University. You will recollect that when I entered upon my labors in the Department of Modern Languages, the special duties, which devolved upon me as Head of that Department, and Professor of Belles Lettres, were agreed upon by a Committee of the Corporation and myself. Native teachers having always been employed to instruct in the elements and pronunciation of the Modern Languages, the general supervision of the Department, instruction in some of the higher works of modern foreign literature, and certain courses of Lectures were assigned to me. This arrangement, so far as I know, proved satisfactory to all the parties concerned.

You will also recollect, that in the Summer of 1838, two gentlemen, namely the French and the German Instructors, for reasons which it is unnecessary to specify, resigned. Another German teacher was immediately appointed; but as no suitable person occurred at the moment to fill the place of French Instructor, the appointment of one was postponed for a season, and I consented to take charge of the Classes in that language. I would respectfully remind you of the distinct understanding at the time, that this arrangement was to be only a temporary one, and to be given up as soon as a suitable appointment could be made. It so happened, however, that I continued to instruct in the French language during the whole year.

At the commencement of the present academical year, I proposed the name of a French gentleman, and this nomination was laid by the President before your honorable body. No appointment, however, was made; but on the contrary a vote was passed, requiring the Smith Professor to instruct all the French classes for the future.

I do not, of course, Gentlemen, call in question your right to modify the duties of my Professorship; and I have proceeded to organize the classes, and commence the instruction in the Elements of the French language, agreeably to your vote. But I still entertain the [hope] that a different arrangement, and one more in harmony with the intent of a Professorship of Belles Lettres, and more advantageous to the University, may yet be made. The symmetry and completeness of the Department are at present destroyed. The organization introduced by Mr. Ticknor, and continued successfully to the great honor of the University is broken up. The French language has no native teacher. And I submit to you, Gentlemen, whether depriving the Department of the services of such a teacher will not justly be regarded by the public as lessening the advantages of a residence at the University.

I have now under my charge 115 students in French, and 30 in German. Of course, with so many pupils my time is fully occupied. I can exercise but little superintendence over the Department; and have no leisure for the prosecution of those studies, which are absolutely requisite for the proper discharge of the duties originally prescribed to me. When the labor of mastering the Literature of even a single nation is considered,--the utter impossibility of my accomplishing anything, under the present arrangement,-- in the various fields of Foreign Literature, over which my Professorship ranges, will be at once apparent. An object of greater importance is clearly sacrificed to one of less. I am required to withdraw from those literary studies and instructions, which had been originally marked out for me, and to devote my time to Elementary Instruction. Now if my labors are of any importance to the College it is to the former class of duties, that the importance belongs. The latter can be performed as well, perhaps better, by an instructor, employed and paid in the usual way. In point of fact, my office as Professor of

Belles Lettres is almost annihilated, and I have become merely a teacher of French. To remedy this, Gentlemen, I make to you the following propositions:--

I. That I should be wholly separated from the Department of Modern Languages, and be only Professor of Belles Lettres.

II. That I should reside, as now, in Cambridge.

III. That I should not be a member of the Faculty.

IV. That my duties be confined to lecturing during the Autumn Term; and the rest of the year be at my own disposal, as in the case of the Professor of History.

V. In consideration of which I relinquish one half of my present income from the College, and receive only one thousand dollars per annum. Respectfully submitted.

HENRY W. LONGFELLOW.{56}

The committee to which was referred the memorial of Professor Longfellow reports:--

That in conformity with his wishes, one of two modifications of his existing duties may be admitted consistently with the interest of the University, both being predicated upon the plan of substituting a native of France as a principal teacher of the French language.

1. That Professor Longfellow's services should be limited to public lectures and oral instruction & relief from all other teaching, & to continue the general superintendence of the Department and to continue his lectures both terms and receive a salary of One Thousand dollars.

2. That he perform the above and give instruction by hearing recitations of the advance Classes in French, in both terms, and also of all the surplus of the Students in French, when their numbers shall exceed One Hundred & to receive a salary of Fifteen hundred dollars.

The committee submit it to the wisdom of the board, which of these modifications is preferable.

For the Committee, 26 Oct. 1839.

JOSIAH QUINCY.{57}

At a later period came the following:--

GENTLEMEN,--I am reluctantly compelled by the state of my health to ask leave of absence from the College for six months from the first of May next. In this time I propose to visit Germany, to try the effect of certain baths, by means of which, as well as by the relaxation and the sea-voyage, I hope to reestablish my health. My medical attendant advises this course as more efficacious than any treatment I can receive at home.

I shall be able, before leaving, to deliver all the lectures of the Spring Term; and on my return in November, those of the Autumn Term before its close; and it is in reference to the necessary arrangements for this, that I make thus early my application for leave of absence. The general supervision of the Department will be undertaken by Professor Felton, without any charge to the College;--the classes will lose none of their lectures;--and I trust the interests of the College will not suffer.

I would repeat in conclusion that the state of my health is the sole reason of my making this request.

I am, Gentlemen, Your Ob't. Ser't.

HENRY W. LONGFELLOW.{58}

HARVARD UNIVERSITY, January 24, 1842. To the President and Fellows of Harvard University.

He sailed on April 23, 1842, and although his health gained during the summer, was yet obliged to ask for an extension of time, as follows:--

MARIENBERG, September 3, 1842.

MY DEAR SIR [Hon. Josiah Quincy],--When I left you in the Spring, I thought by this time I should have recovered my health and be setting my face homeward. In this I have been disappointed. My recovery has been slower than I expected; and though considerably better than when I arrived here, I am yet far from being well. The Doctor urges me very strongly to remain longer. He thinks it of the utmost importance to my future health, for years to come, that I should do so. He says, that if I look forward to a life of intellectual labor, in his opinion "it is absolutely necessary I should give up all thought of returning home before next Summer, devoting the time to reestablishing my health, and avoiding all severe study." I quote these words from a written opinion which he gave me this morning; and in consequence of which I have determined to ask leave of absence until that time, unless the state of my department in College should absolutely demand my return.

I assure you, that I do this with the greatest reluctance. I have no desire to remain here; on the contrary a very strong desire to be at home and at work. Still I wish to return in good health and spirits, and not to lead a maimed life. I fear, and the physician positively asserts, that if I go back now I shall thwart the whole object of my journey, and that if I hope to be well I must go on with the baths.

I have therefore concluded to remain here until I receive an answer from you; promising myself that when I once escape from this hospital I will never enter another until that final one appointed for all the poets.

Will you have the goodness to say to your daughter, Miss Quincy, that I left her package for Mr. Graham at its address in Havre; and presume it reached him safely. In coming through France it was not in my power to go into Brittany, and avail myself of your letter of introduction to him; the place of his residence lying too far out of my route. From Paris I came through Belgium to this ancient city of Boppard, where I have remained stationary since the first of June.

With kind remembrances to Mrs. Quincy and your family,

Very truly yours

HENRY W. LONGFELLOW.{59}

It is interesting to note the manner in which this appeal was met by the economical college.

HENRY W. LONGFELLOW, ESQ.

SIR,--I perceive with great regret, by your letter of the 3d Inst. that, although you have followed with due precision the prescriptions of the German Doctor who

corpus recenti sparget aqua,

convalescence is not yet attained, but that the water spirit has announced that another year is required in order to obtain the full benefit of his draughts and ablutions. The fact is a source of great sorrow to your friends and of no less embarrassment to the Corporation of the College. The granting the leave of six months' absence was effected, not without difficulty. Doubts were expressed concerning the possibility of your realizing your expectations, within the period you specified; and the objections were surmounted only on your assurance that you would return in October, and that the benefit of your instructions should not be lost, by any [class] of the college, according to the arrangements you made. It was on this fact, and on this assurance alone, that assent of the Corporation was obtained. By the proposition you now make the present Senior class will be deprived of the advantages, on which they have a right to calculate and have been taught to expect.

Under the circumstances of the case, the Corporation do not feel themselves willing absolutely to withhold their assent to your protracting your absence as you propose; at the same time they are compelled by their sense of duty & I am authorized to state, that they, regarding themselves, not as proprietors, but as trustees, of the funds under their control, cannot deem themselves justified in paying the salary of the Professorship to a Professor, not resident & not performing its duties. They value your services very highly, and are therefore willing, if you see fit to remain another year in Europe, to keep the Professorship open for your return; but I am directed to say that, in such case, your salary must cease, at the end of the current quarter--viz. on the 30 of November next.

The obligation thus imposed on the Corporation, it is very painful to them to fulfil, but they cannot otherwise execute the trust they have undertaken, conformably to their sense of duty.

And now, Sir, permit me to express my best wishes for your health; the high sense I entertain of your talents and attainments and the unaltered esteem & respect with which I am, most truly.

Your friend and hl'e S't.

JOSIAH QUINCY.{60}

CAMBRIDGE. 30. Sep. 1842.

Longfellow spent his summer at the water-cure in Marienberg, with some diverging trips, as those to Paris, Antwerp, and Bruges. In Paris he took a letter to Jules Janin, now pretty well forgotten, but then the foremost critic in Paris, who disliked the society of literary men, saying that he never saw them and never wished to see them; and who had quarrelled personally with all the French authors, except Lamartine, whom he pronounced "as good as an angel." In Bruges the young traveller took delight in the belfry, and lived to transmit some of its charms to others. At Antwerp he had the glories of the cathedral, the memory of Quintin Matsys, and the paintings of Rubens. His home at Marienberg was in an ancient cloister for noble nuns, converted into a water-cure, then a novelty and much severer in its discipline than its later copies in America, to one of which, however, Longfellow himself went later as a patient,--that of Dr. Wesselhoeft at Brattleboro, Vermont. He met or read German poets also,--Becker, Herwegh, Lenau, Auersberg, Zedlitz, and Freiligrath, with the latter of whom he became intimate; indeed reading aloud to admiring nuns his charming poem about "The Flowers' Revenge" (Der Blumen Rache). He just missed seeing Uhland, the only German poet then more popular than Freiligrath; he visited camps of 50,000 troops and another camp of naturalists at Mayence. Meantime, he heard from Prescott, Sumner, and Felton at home; the "Spanish Student" went through the press, and his friend Hawthorne was married. He finally sailed for home on October 22, 1842, and occupied himself on the voyage in writing a small volume of poems on slavery.

{56 Harvard College Papers [MS.], 2d ser. ix. 318.}

{57 Harvard College Papers [MS.], 2d ser. ix. 336.}

{58 Harvard College Papers [MS.], 2d ser. x. 363.}

{59 Harvard College Papers [MS.], 2d ser. xi. 153.}

{60 Harvard College Papers [MS.], 2d ser. xi. 187.}

CHAPTER XIV

ANTI-SLAVERY POEMS AND SECOND MARRIAGE

It is difficult now to realize what an event in Longfellow's life was the fact of his writing a series of anti-slavery poems on board ship and publishing them in a thin pamphlet on his return. Parties on the subject were already strongly drawn; the anti-slavery party being itself divided into subdivisions which criticised each other sharply. Longfellow's temperament was thoroughly gentle and shunned extremes, so that the little thin yellow-covered volume came upon the community with something like a shock. As a matter of fact, various influences had led him up to it. His father had been a subscriber to Benjamin Lundy's "Genius of Universal Emancipation," the precursor of Garrison's "Liberator." In his youth at Brunswick, Longfellow had thought of writing a drama on the subject of "Toussaint l'Ouverture," his reason for it being thus given, "that thus I may do something in my humble way for the great cause of negro emancipation."

Margaret Fuller, who could by no means be called an abolitionist, described the volume as "the thinnest of all Mr. Longfellow's thin books; spirited and polished like its forerunners; but the subject would warrant a deeper tone." On the other hand, the editors of "Graham's Magazine" wrote to Mr. Longfellow that "the word slavery was never allowed to appear in a Philadelphia periodical," and that "the publisher objected to have even the name of the book appear in his pages." His friend Samuel Ward, always an agreeable man of the world, wrote from New York of the poems, "They excite a good deal of attention and sell rapidly. I have sent one copy to the South and others shall follow," and includes Longfellow among "you abolitionists." The effect of the poems was unquestionably to throw him on the right side of the great moral contest then rising to its climax, while he incurred, like his great compeers, Channing, Emerson, and Sumner, some criticism from the pioneers. Such differences are inevitable among reformers, whose internal contests are apt to be more strenuous and formidable than those incurred between opponents; and recall to mind that remark of Cosmo de Medici which Lord Bacon called "a desperate saying;" namely, that "Holy Writ bids us to forgive our enemies, but it is nowhere enjoined upon us that we should forgive our friends."

To George Lunt, a poet whose rhymes Longfellow admired, but who bitterly opposed the anti-slavery movement, he writes his programme as follows:--

"I am sorry you find so much to gainsay in my Poems on Slavery. I shall not argue the point with you, however, but will simply state to you my belief.

"1. I believe slavery to be an unrighteous institution, based on the false maxim that Might makes Right.

"2. I have great faith in doing what is righteous, and fear no evil consequences.

"3. I believe that every one has a perfect right to express his opinion on the subject of Slavery, as on every other thing; that every one ought so to do, until the public opinion of all Christendom shall penetrate into and change the hearts of the Southerners on this subject.

"4. I would have no other interference than what is sanctioned by law.

"5. I believe that where there is a will there is a way. When the whole country sincerely wishes to get rid of Slavery, it will readily find the means.

"6. Let us, therefore, do all we can to bring about this will, in all gentleness and Christian charity.

"And God speed the time!"{61}

Mr. Longfellow was, I think, not quite justly treated by the critics, or even by his latest biographer, Professor Carpenter,{62} for consenting to the omission of the anti-slavery poems from his works, published by Carey and Hart in Philadelphia in November, 1845. This was an illustrated edition which had been for some time in preparation and did not apparently, like the nearly simultaneous edition of Harper, assume to contain his complete works. The Harper edition was published in February, 1846, in cheaper form and double columns, and was the really collective edition, containing the anti-slavery poems and all. As we do not know the circumstances of the case, it cannot positively be asserted why this variation occurred, but inasmuch as the Harpers were at that period, and for many years after, thoroughly conservative on the slavery question and extremely opposed to referring to it in any way, it is pretty certain that it must have been because of the positive demand of Longfellow that these poems were included by them. The criticism of the abolitionists on him was undoubtedly strengthened by the apostrophe to the Union at the close of his poem, "The Building of the Ship," in 1850, a passage which was described by William Lloyd Garrison in the "Liberator" as "a eulogy dripping with the blood of imbruted humanity,"{63} and was quite as severely viewed by one of the most zealous of the Irish abolitionists, who thus wrote to their friends in Boston:--

DUBLIN [IRELAND], April 28, 1850.

[After speaking about Miss Weston's displeasure with Whittier and her being unfair to him, etc., the letter adds--]

Is it not a poor thing for Longfellow that he is no abolitionist--that his anti-slavery poetry is perfect dish water beside Whittier's--and that he has just penned a Paen on the Union? I can no more comprehend what there is in the Union to make the Yankee nation adore it--than you can understand the attractions of Royalty & Aristocracy which thousands of very good people in England look on as the source & mainstay of all that is great and good in the nation....

RICH D. WEBB.{64}

Yet Mr. Whittier himself, though thus contrasted with Longfellow, had written thanking him for his "Poems on Slavery," which in tract form, he said, "had been of important service to the Liberty movement." Whittier had also asked whether Longfellow would accept a nomination to Congress from the Liberty Party, and had added, "Our friends think they could throw for thee one thousand more votes than for any other man."{65} Nor was Whittier himself ever a disunionist, even on anti-slavery grounds.

It is interesting to note that it was apparently the anti-slavery question which laid the foundation for the intimacy between Longfellow and Lowell. Lowell had been invited, on the publication of "A Year's Life," to write for an annual which was to appear in Boston and to be edited, in Lowell's own phrase, "by Longfellow, Felton, Hillard and that set."{66} Lowell subsequently wrote in the "Pioneer" kindly notices of Longfellow's "Poems on Slavery," but there is no immediate evidence of any personal relations between them at that time. In a letter to Poe, dated at Elmwood June 27, 1844, Lowell says of a recent article in the "Foreign Quarterly Review" attributed to John Forster, "Forster is a friend of some of the Longfellow clique here, which perhaps accounts for his putting L. at the top of our Parnassus. These kinds of arrangements do very well, however, for the present."{67}... It will be noticed that what Lowell had originally called a "set" has now become a "clique." It is also evident that lie did not regard Longfellow as the assured head of the American Parnassus, and at any rate he suggests some possible rearrangement for the future. Their real friendship seems to have begun with a visit by Longfellow to Lowell's study on October 29, 1846, when the conversation turned chiefly on the slavery question. Longfellow called to see him again on the publication of his second volume of poems, at the end of the following year, and Lowell spent an evening with Longfellow during March, 1848, while engaged on "The Fable for Critics," in which the younger poet praised the elder so warmly.

Longfellow's own state of mind at this period is well summed up in the following letter to his wife's younger sister, Mrs. Peter Thacher, then recently a mother.

CAMBRIDGE, Feb. 15, 1843.

MY DEAR MARGARET,--I was very much gratified by your brief epistle, which reached me night before last, and brought me the assurances of your kind remembrance. Believe me, I have often thought of you and your husband; and have felt that your new home, though remote from many of your earlier friends, was nevertheless to you the centre of a world of happiness. With your affection, and your "young Astyanax," the "yellow house" becomes a golden palace.

For my part, Life seems to be to me "a battle and a march." I am sometimes well,--sometimes ill, and always restless. My late expedition to Germany did me a vast deal of good; and my health is better than it has been for years. So long as I keep out of doors and take exercise enough, I feel perfectly well. So soon as I shut myself up and begin to study, I feel perfectly ill. Thus the Sphinx's riddle--the secret of health--is discovered. In Germany I led an out-of-door life; bathing and walking from morning till night. I was at Boppard on the Rhine, in the old convent of Marienberg, now a Bathing establishment. I travelled a little in Germany; then passed through Belgium to England. In London I staid with Dickens; and had a very pleasant visit. His wife is a gentle, lovely character; and he has four children, all beautiful and good. I saw likewise the raven, who is stuffed in the entry--and his successor, who stalks gravely in the garden.

I am very sorry, my dear Margaret, that I cannot grant your request in regard to Mary's Journal. Just before I sailed for Europe, being in low spirits, and reflecting on the uncertainties of such an expedition as I was then beginning, I burned a great many letters and private papers, and among them this. I now regret it; but alas! too late.

Ah! my dear Margaret! though somewhat wayward and restless, I most affectionately cherish the memory of my wife. You know how happily we lived together; and I know that never again shall I be loved with such devotion, sincerity, and utter forgetfulness of self. Make her your model, and you will make your husband ever happy; and be to him as a household lamp irradiating his darkest hours.

Give my best regards to him. I should like very much to visit you; but know not how I can bring it about. Kiss "young Astyanax" for me, and believe me ever affectionately your brother

HENRY W. LONGFELLOW.

Meanwhile a vast change in his life was approaching. He had met, seven years before in Switzerland, a maiden of nineteen, Frances Elizabeth Appleton, daughter of Nathan Appleton, a Boston merchant; and though his early sketch of her in "Hyperion" may have implied little on either side, it was fulfilled at any rate, after these years of acquaintance, by her consenting; to become his wife, an event which took place on the 13th of July, 1843, and was thus announced by him in a letter to Miss Eliza A. Potter of Portland, his first wife's elder sister.

CAMBRIDGE, May 25, 1843.

MY DEAR ELIZA,--I have been meaning for a week or more to write you in order to tell you of my engagement, and to ask your sympathies and good wishes. But I have been so much occupied, and have had so many letters to write, to go by the last steamers, that I have been rather neglectful of some of my nearer and dearer friends; trusting to their kindness for my excuse.

Yes, my dear Eliza, I am to be married again. My life was too lonely and restless;--I needed the soothing influences of a home;--and I have chosen a person for my wife who possesses in a high degree those virtues and excellent traits of character, which so distinguished my dear Mary. Think not, that in this new engagement, I do any wrong to her memory. I still retain, and ever shall preserve with sacred care all my cherished recollections of her truth, affection and beautiful nature. And I feel, that could she speak to me, she would approve of what I am doing. I hope also for your approval and for your father's.... Think of me ever as

Very truly your friend

HENRY W. LONGFELLOW.{68}

The lady thus described was one who lives in the memory of all who knew her, were it only by her distinguished appearance and bearing, her "deep, unutterable eyes," in Longfellow's own phrase, and her quiet, self-controlled face illumined by a radiant smile. She was never better described, perhaps, than by the Hungarian, Madame Pulszky, who visited America with Kossuth, and who wrote of her as "a lady of Junonian beauty and of the kindest heart."{69} Promptly and almost insensibly she identified herself with all her husband's work, a thing rendered peculiarly valuable from the fact that his eyes had become overstrained, so that he welcomed an amanuensis. Sometimes she suggested subjects for poems, this being at least the case with "The Arsenal at Springfield," first proposed by her within the very walls of the building, a spot whose moral was doubtless enhanced by the companionship of Charles Sumner, just then the especial prophet of international peace. She also aided him effectually in his next book, "The Poets and Poetry of Europe," in which his friend Felton also cooperated, he preparing the biographical notices while Longfellow made the selections and also some of the translations.

I add this letter from his betrothed, which strikes the reader as singularly winning and womanly. This also is addressed to the elder sister of the first Mrs. Longfellow.

BOSTON, June 5, 1843.

DEAR MISS POTTER,--Accept my warmest thanks for the very kind manner in which you have expressed an interest in our happiness. It is all the more welcome in coming from a stranger upon whom I have no past claim to kindle a kindly regard, and touches my heart deeply. Among the many blessings which the new world I have entered reveals to me, a new heritage of friends is a choice one. Those most dear to Henry, most closely linked with his early associations, I am, naturally, most anxious to know and love,--and I trust an opportunity will bring us together before long.

But I should feel no little timidity in being known to you and his family; a dread that loving him as you do I might not fulfil all the exactions of your hearts; were not such fears relieved by the generous determination you have shown to approve his choice,--upon faith in him. To one who has known him so long and so well, I need not attempt to speak of my happiness in possessing such a heart,--nor of my infinite gratitude to the Giver of every good gift for bestowing upon me the power of rendering him once more happy in the hope of a home,--so sacred and dear to his loving nature by blessed memories to which I fervently pray to be found worthy to succeed.

Receive again my thanks for your kind sympathy, with the assurance of my warm regards,--which I trust will not always be imprisoned in words, and with kindest remembrances to my other Portland friends,

I remain sincerely and gratefully yrs

FANNY E. APPLETON.

Henry sends his most affectionate regards and hopes, tho' faintly, to be soon able to visit his home, and talk over his future with you all.{70}

It is pleasant to record in connection with this sweet and high-minded letter, that a copy of "Hyperion" itself lies before me which is inscribed on the first page in pencil to "Miss Eliza A. Potter, from her affectionate friend and brother, the Author." That he preserved through life a warm friendliness toward all the kindred of his first wife is quite certain.

{61 Life, ii. 8.}

{62 Beacon Biographies (Longfellow), p. 77.}

{63 Garrison's Memoirs, iii. 280.}

{64 Western MSS., Boston Public Library.}

{65 Life, ii. 20.}

{66 Scudder's Lowell, i. 93.}

{67 Correspondence of R. W. Griswold, p. 151.}

{68 MS.}

{69 White, Red, and Black, ii. 237.}

{70 MS.}

CHAPTER XV

There exists abundant evidence, to which the present writer can add personal testimony, in regard to Longfellow's success as an organizer of his immediate department of Harvard University and in dealing with his especial classes. He was assigned, for some reason, a room in University Hall which was also employed for faculty meetings, and was therefore a little less dreary than the ordinary class-room of those days. It seemed most appropriate that an instructor of Longfellow's well-bred aspect and ever-courteous manners should simply sit at the head of the table with his scholars, as if they were guests, instead of putting between him and them the restrictive demarcation of a teacher's desk. We read with him, I remember, first the little book he edited, "Proverbes Dramatiques," and afterwards something of Racine and Moliere, in which his faculty of finding equivalent phrases was an admirable example for us. When afterwards, during an abortive rebellion in the college yard, the students who had refused to listen to others yielded to the demand of their ringleader, "Let us hear Professor Longfellow; he always treats us like gentlemen," the youthful rebel unconsciously recognized a step forward in academical discipline. Longfellow did not cultivate us much personally, or ask us to his house, but he remembered us and acknowledged our salutations. He was, I think, the first Harvard instructor who addressed the individual student with the prefix "Mr." I recall the clearness of his questions, the simplicity of his explanations, the well-bred and skilful propriety with which he led us past certain indiscreet phrases in our French authors, as for instance in Balzac's "Peau de Chagrin." Most of all comes back to memory the sense of triumph with which we saw the proof-sheets of "Voices of the Night" brought in by the printer's devil and laid at his elbow. We felt that we also had lived in literary society, little dreaming, in our youthful innocence, how large a part of such society would prove far below the standard of courtesy that prevailed in Professor Longfellow's recitation room.

Yet the work of this room was, in those days of dawning changes, but a small part of the function of a professor. Longfellow was, both by inclination and circumstances, committed to the reform initiated by his predecessor, George Ticknor. He had inherited from this predecessor a sort of pioneership in position relative to the elective system just on trial as an experiment in college. There exists an impression in some quarters that this system came in for the first time under President Walker about 1853; but it had been, as a matter of fact, tried much earlier,--twenty years, at least,--in the Modern Language Department under Ticknor, and had been extended much more widely in 1839 under President Quincy. The facts are well known to me, as I was in college at that period and enjoyed the beneficent effects of the change, since it placed the whole college, in some degree, for a time at least, on a university basis. The change took the form, first, of a discontinuance of mathematics as a required study after the first year, and then the wider application of the elective system in history, natural history, and the classics, this greater liberty being enjoyed, though with some reaction, under President Everett, and practically abolished about 1849 under President Sparks, when what may be called the High School system was temporarily restored. An illustration of this reactionary tendency may be found in a letter addressed by Longfellow to the President and Fellows, placing him distinctly on the side of freedom of choice. The circumstances are these: Students had for some time been permitted to take more than one modern language among the electives, and I myself, before receiving my degree of A. B. in 1841, had studied two such languages simultaneously for three years of college course. It appears, however, from the following letter, that this privilege had already been reduced to one such language, and that Longfellow was at once found remonstrating against it, though at first ineffectually.

CAMBRIDGE, June 24, 1845.

GENTLEMEN,--In arranging the studies for the next year, the Faculty have voted, as will be seen from the enclosed Tabular view, that "no student will be allowed to take more than one Modern Language at a time, except for special reasons assigned, & by express vote of the Faculty."

You will see that this is the only Department upon which any bar or prohibition is laid. And when the decision was made, the Latin & Greek Departments were allowed two votes each, & the Department of Modern Languages but one vote.

As I foresaw at the time, this arrangement has proved very disadvantageous to the Department, & has reduced the number of pupils, at once, more than one half. During this year the whole number of students in the Department has been 224. The applications for the next term do not amount to 100; nor, when all have been received, can it reach 110. I therefore, Gentlemen, appeal to you, for your interference in this matter, requesting that the restriction may be removed, & this Department put upon the footing of the others in this particular. Otherwise, I fear that as at present organized, it cannot exist another year.

I have the honor to be, Gentlemen, your ob'd't. servant

HENRY W. LONGFELLOW.{71}

[Addressed externally to the President and Fellows of Harvard College.]

[REPORT OF COMMITTEE.]

CORPORATION OF HARVARD COLLEGE, July 26, 1845.

The Committee to whom was referred the Memorial of Professor Longfellow on the subject of the arrangement of the studies of the undergraduates by the faculty of the College, & desiring that the restriction as to the number of modern languages that may be studied at once should be removed, have attended to the subject, & ask leave to report, that they have, in common with the other members of the Corporation already considered the general subject of the arrangement of the studies of the undergraduates, with especial reference to the recommendations of the board of overseers; & that they were convinced by the examination of the details they made at that time that the business of ordering the times & the amount of study & recitation for the young men at Cambridge is not only a very complicated & difficult affair, but one which is in the hands of those best qualified, & considering all their relations, most truly interested to lead the students to give as much labor as is safe for them to the studies suitable to College years, & to distribute it in such manner as shall be most just & effective. The committee would not feel themselves authorized to change one part of a system, all the parts of which are intricately dependent upon each other, without they felt a confidence they do not possess that they could recommend one which should work better as a whole. They therefore must decline, so far as depends upon them, adopting a measure the ulterior effects of which they may not foresee with accuracy, & they express the belief that it will be well to allow the present arrangement to continue for a time, even at the risk, apprehended by Prof'r. Longfellow, of its producing an injurious effect upon his department. They cannot but hope, however, that the evils he fears may be avoided, or if not, that they may be compensated by equivalent advantages.

SAM'L. A. ELIOT \ } Committee{72} J. A. LOWELL /

A year later than the above correspondence, the subject was evidently revived on the part of the governing powers of the College, and we find the following letter from Professor Longfellow:--

CAMBRIDGE, Sept. 25, 1846.

DEAR SIR,--In answer to your favor of the 18th inst. requesting my opinion on certain points connected with the Studies of the University, I beg leave to state;

I. In regard to the "advantages and disadvantages of the Elective System." In my own department I have always been strongly in favor of this system. I have always thought that the modern languages should be among the voluntary or elective studies and form no part of the required Academic course. As to the Latin and Greek I have many doubts; but incline rather to the old system, particularly if the fifth class can be added to the present course; for we could then secure the advantages of both systems.

II. The class examinations in my department are very slight and unsatisfactory. They serve however as a kind of Annual Report of what has been done in the department; and as there is nothing depending upon them, it does not seem to me a matter of very urgent necessity to have them rendered more thorough.

III. "The Fifth class or New Department in the University" seems to me of the greatest importance, as it would enable us to carry forward the studies of each department much farther than at present, by means of Lectures, for which there is now hardly sufficient opportunity. Last year there were fifteen Resident Graduates. Why should not these have formed the Fifth Class?

IV. In regard to the "practical working of any other of the changes made in our system during the last twenty years," I can hardly claim any distinct views. Many, perhaps most of them were made before I came to the University; so that I hardly know what is old and what is new.

I have made but a brief statement in answer to your enquiries, partly because writing is a painful process with me, and partly because many things here touched upon can be more clearly explained vive voce than with the pen.

I remain, with great regard Faithfully Yours

HENRY W. LONGFELLOW.{73}

It is a curious fact that more than half a century later, at a meeting of the American Modern Language Association, held at the very institution where this correspondence took place, it was President Charles William Eliot, son of the author of the letter just quoted, who recognized the immense advance made in this particular department as one of the most important steps in the progress of the University. His remarks were thus reported in the Boston "Herald" of December 27, 1901:--

"When the meeting opened yesterday afternoon President Eliot was present and graciously said a few words of welcome. He said that he knew of no body of modern learned men whom he would be so glad to welcome as the professors of language.

"'Here at Harvard,' he said, 'we have been pressing forward for many years toward the same object you have in view. I congratulate you upon the great progress made in the last thirty years. One of the most striking features of American education has been the rapid development of the study of languages. It has been more rapid at some of the other colleges than at Harvard. They started at nothing a shorter time ago. [Laughter.]

"'You are to be congratulated upon the cohesion which exists among learned men in dealing with this important subject. The study of modern languages is beginning to connect itself with the life of the nation. It now bears a real connection to national life and interest. No great subject in educational thought ever obtained a firm hold that had not some modern connection with the day. I do not overlook the literary element in the study of modern languages, but you will have a stronger hold for the next twenty years than you have in the past, owing to this use of modern languages in daily life, incident to the industrial and commercial activity of the country.'"

It is always to be borne in mind that Longfellow's self-restrained and well-ordered temperament habitually checked him in the career of innovator. Both in public and private matters, it was his way to state his point of view and then await results. It is clear that his mental habit, his foreign experience, and the traditions of his immediate department predisposed him to favor the elective system in university training. This system, after temporary trial and abandonment, was now being brought forward once more and was destined this time to prevail. Towards this success, the prosperity of the Modern Language Department formed a perpetual argument, because it was there that the reform was first introduced. The records of the Faculty at that period give very little information as to the attitude of individual professors, and Longfellow may be viewed as having been for the most part a silent reformer. One finds, however, constant evidence in his diaries of the fact that his duties wore upon him. "I get very tired of the routine of this life." "This college work is like a great hand laid on all the strings of my lyre, stopping their vibrations." "How the days resemble each other and how sad it is to me that I cannot give them all to my poem." "I have fallen into a very unpoetic mood and cannot write." It must be remembered that his eyes were at this time very weak, that he suffered extremely from neuralgia, and that these entries were all made during the great fugitive slave excitement which agitated New England, and the political overturn in Massachusetts which culminated in the election of the poet's most intimate friend, Sumner, to the United States Senate. He records the occurrence of his forty-fourth birthday, and soon after when he is stereotyping the "Golden Legend" he says: "I still work a good deal upon it," but also writes, only two days after, "Working hard with college classes to have them ready for their examinations." A fortnight later he says: "Examination in my department; always to me a day of anguish and exhaustion." His correspondence is very large; visitors and dinner parties constantly increase. His mother dies suddenly, and he sits all night alone by her dead body; a sense of peace comes over him, as if there had been no shock or jar in nature, but a "harmonious close to a long life." Later he gets tired of summer rest at Nahant, which he calls "building up life with solid blocks of idleness;" but when two days later he goes back to Cambridge to resume his duties, he records: "I felt my neck bow and the pressure of the yoke." Soon after he says: "I find no time to write. I find more and more the little things of life shut out the great. Innumerable interruptions--letters of application for this and for that; endless importunities of foreigners for help here and help there--fret the day and consume it." He often records having half a dozen men to dine with him; he goes to the theatre, to lectures, concerts, and balls, has no repose, and perhaps, as we have seen at Nahant, would not really enjoy it. It was under these conditions, however, that the "Golden Legend" came into the world in November, 1851; and it was not until September 12, 1854, that its author was finally separated from the University. He was before that date happily at work on "Hiawatha."

{71 Harvard College Papers [MS.], 2d ser. xiii. 363.}

{72 Harvard College Papers [MS.], 2d ser. xiii. 13.}

{73 Harvard College Papers [MSS.], 2d ser. xiv. 61.}

CHAPTER XVI

LITERARY LIFE IN CAMBRIDGE

Let us now return from the history of Longfellow's academic life to his normal pursuit, literature. It seemed a curious transition from the real and genuine sympathy for human wrong, as shown in the "Poems on Slavery," to the purely literary and historic quality of the "Spanish Student" (1843), a play never quite dramatic enough to be put on the stage, at least in English, though a German version was performed at the Ducal Court Theatre in Dessau, January 28, 1855. As literary work it was certainly well done; though taken in part from the tale of Cervantes "La Gitanilla," and handled before by Montalvan and by Solis in Spanish, and by Middleton in English, it yet was essentially Longfellow's own in treatment, though perhaps rather marred by taking inappropriately the motto from Robert Burns. He wrote of it to Samuel Ward in New York, December, 1840, calling it "something still longer which as yet no eye but mine has seen and which I wish to read to you first." He then adds, "At present, my dear friend, my soul is wrapped up in poetry. The scales fell from my eyes suddenly, and I beheld before me a beautiful landscape, with figures, which I have transferred to paper almost without an effort, and with a celerity of which I did not think myself capable. Since my return from Portland I am almost afraid to look at it, for fear its colors should have faded out. And this is the reason why I do not describe the work to you more particularly. I am not sure it is worth it. You shall yourself see and judge before long." He thus afterwards describes it to his father: "I have also written a much longer and more difficult poem, called 'The Spanish Student,'--a drama in five acts; on the success of which I rely with some self-complacency. But this is a great secret, and must not go beyond the immediate family circle; as I do not intend to publish it until the glow of composition has passed away, and I can look upon it coolly and critically. I will tell you more of this by and by."

Longfellow's work on "The Poets and Poetry of Europe" appeared in 1845, and was afterwards reprinted with a supplement in 1871. The original work included 776 pages,{74} the supplement adding 340 more. The supplement is in some respects better edited than the original, because it gives the names of the translators, and because he had some better translators to draw upon, especially Rossetti. It can be said fairly of the whole book that it is intrinsically one of the most attractive of a very unattractive class, a book of which the compiler justly says that, in order to render the literary history of the various countries complete, "an author of no great note has sometimes been admitted, or a poem which a severer taste would have excluded." "The work is to be regarded," he adds, "as a collection, rather than as a selection, and in judging any author it must be borne in mind the translations do not always preserve the rhythm and melody of the original, but often resemble soldiers moving forward when the music has ceased and the time is marked only by the tap of the drum." It includes, in all, only ten languages, the Celtic and Slavonic being excluded, as well as the Turkish and Romaic, a thing which would now seem strange. But the editor's frank explanation of the fact, where he says "with these I am not acquainted," disarms criticism. This explanation implies that he was personally acquainted with the six Gothic languages of Northern Europe--Anglo-Saxon, Icelandish, Danish, Swedish, German, and Dutch--and the four Latin languages of the South of Europe--French, Italian, Spanish, and Portuguese. The mere work of compiling so large a volume in double columns of these ten languages was something formidable, and he had reason to be grateful to his friend Professor Felton, who, being a German student, as well as a Greek scholar, compiled for him all the biographical notes in the book. It is needless to say that the selection is as good as the case permitted or as the plan of the book allowed, and the volume has always maintained its place of importance in libraries. Many of the translations were made expressly for it, especially in the supplement;

among these being Platen's "Remorse," Reboul's "The Angel and Child," and Malherbe's "Consolation." It is to be remembered that Longfellow's standard of translation was very high and that he always maintained, according to Mrs. Fields, that Americans, French, and Germans had a greater natural gift for it than the English on account of the greater insularity of the latter's natures.{75} It is also to be noted that he sometimes failed to find material for translation where others found it, as, for instance, amid the endless beauty of the Greek Anthology, which he called "the most melancholy of books with an odor of dead garlands about it. Voices from the grave, cymbals of Bacchantes, songs of love, sighs, groans, prayers,--all mingled together. I never read a book that made me sadder."{76}

His fame at this time was widely established, yet a curious indication of the fact that he did not at once take even Cambridge by storm, as a poet, is in a letter from Professor Andrews Norton, father of the present Professor Charles E. Norton, to the Rev. W. H. Furness of Philadelphia. The latter had apparently applied to Mr. Norton for advice as to a desirable list of American authors from whom to make some literary selections, perhaps in connection with an annual then edited by him and called "The Diadem." Professor Norton, as one of the most cultivated Americans, might naturally be asked for some such counsel. In replying he sent Mr. Furness, under date of January 7, 1845, a list of fifty-four eligible authors, among whom Emerson stood last but one, while Longfellow was not included at all. He then appended a supplementary list of twenty-four minor authors, headed by Longfellow.{77} We have already seen Lowell, from a younger point of view, describing Longfellow, at about this time, as the head of a "clique," and we now find Andrews Norton, from an older point of view, assigning him only the first place among authors of the second grade. It is curious to notice, in addition, that Hawthorne stood next to Longfellow in this subordinate roll.

Longfellow published two volumes of poetic selections, "The Waif" (1845) and "The Estray" (1846), the latter title being originally planned as "Estrays in the Forest," and he records a visit to the college library, in apparent search for the origin of the phrase. His next volume of original poems, however, was "The Belfry of Bruges and Other Poems," published December 23, 1845, the contents having already been partly printed in "Graham's Magazine," and most of them in the illustrated edition of his poems published in Philadelphia. The theme of the volume appears to have been partly suggested by some words in a letter to Freiligrath which seem to make the leading poem, together with that called "Nuremberg," a portion of that projected series of travel-sketches which had haunted Longfellow ever since "Outre-Mer." "The Norman Baron" was the result of a passage from Thierry, sent him by an unknown correspondent. One poem was suggested by a passage in Andersen's "Story of my Life," and one was written at Boppard on the Rhine. All the rest were distinctly American in character or origin. Another poem, "To the Driving Cloud," the chief of the Omaha Indians, was his first effort at hexameters and prepared the way for "Evangeline." His translation of the "Children of the Lord's Supper" had also served by way of preparation; and he had happened upon a specimen in "Blackwood's Magazine" of the hexameter translation of the "Iliad" which had impressed him very much. He even tried a passage of "Evangeline" rendered into English pentameter verse, and thus satisfied himself that it was far less effective for his purpose than the measure finally adopted.

There is no doubt that the reading public at large has confirmed the opinion of Dr. Oliver Wendell Holmes when he says, "Of the longer poems of our chief singer, I should not hesitate to select 'Evangeline' as the masterpiece, and I think the general verdict of opinion would confirm my choice.... From the first line of the poem, from its first words, we read as we would float down a broad and placid river, murmuring softly against its banks, heaven over it, and the glory of the unspoiled wilderness all around." The words "This is the forest primeval" have become as familiar, he thinks, as the "Arma virumque cano" which opened Virgil's "Æneid," and he elsewhere calls the poem "the tranquil current of these brimming, slow-moving, soul-satisfying lines." The subject was first suggested to Longfellow by Hawthorne, who had heard it from his friend, the Rev. H. L. Conolly, and the outline of it will be found in "The American Note-Books" of Hawthorne, who disappointed Father Conolly by not using it himself. It was finished on Longfellow's fortieth birthday.

It was a striking illustration of the wide popularity of "Evangeline," that even the proper names introduced under guidance of his rhythmical ear spread to other countries and were taken up and preserved as treasures in themselves. Sumner writes from England to Longfellow that the Hon. Mrs. Norton, herself well known in literature, had read "Evangeline," not once only, but twenty times, and the scene on Lake Atchafalaya, where the two lovers pass each other unknowingly, so impressed her that she had a seal cut with the name upon it. Not long after this, Leopold, King of the Belgiums, repeated the same word to her and said that it was so suggestive of scenes in human life that he was about to have it cut on a seal, when she astonished him by showing him hers.

The best review of "Evangeline" ever written was probably the analysis made of it by that accomplished French traveller," published in 1851. It is interesting to read it, and to recognize anew what has often been made manifest--the greater acuteness of the French mind than of the English, when discussing American themes. Writing at that early period, M. Chasles at once recognized, for instance, the peculiar quality of Emerson's genius. He describes Longfellow, in comparison, as what he calls a moonlight poet, having little passion, but a calmness of attitude which approaches majesty, and moreover a deep sensibility, making itself felt under a subdued rhythm. In short, his is a slow melody and a reflective emotion, both these being well suited to the sounds and shadows of our endless plains and our forests, which have no history. He is especially struck with the resemblance of the American poet to the Scandinavians, such as Tegn and Oehlenschlaeger. He notices even in Longfellow the Norse tendency to alliteration, and he quotes one of the Northern poems and then one of Longfellow's to show this analogy. It is worth while to put these side by side. This is from Oehlenschlaeger:--

"Tilgiv tvungne Trael af Elskov! At han dig atter Astsaeld findet." ... etc.

The following is by Longfellow:--

"Fuller of fragrance, than they And as heavy with shadows and night-dews, Hung the heart of the maiden. The calm and magical moonlight Seemed to inundate her soul."

It is curious to notice that Chasles makes the same criticism on "Evangeline" that Holmes made on Lowell's "Vision of Sir Launfal;" namely, that there is in it a mixture of the artificial and the natural. The result is, we may infer, that on the whole one still thinks of it as a work of art and does not--as, for instance, with Tolstoi's "Cossacks"--think of all the characters as if they lived in the very next street. Yet it is in its way so charming, he finds that although as he says, "There is no passion in it," still there is a perpetual air of youth and innocence and tenderness. M. Chasles is also impressed as a Catholic with the poet's wide and liberal comprehension of the Christian ideas. It is not, he thinks, a masterpiece (Il y a loin d'Evangenine ?un chef-d'oeuvre), but he points out, what time has so far vindicated, that it has qualities which guarantee to it something like immortality. When we consider that Chasles wrote at a time when all our more substantial literature seemed to him to consist of uninteresting state histories and extensive collections of the correspondence of American presidents--a time when he could write sadly: "All America does not yet possess a humorist" (Toute l'Amerique ne posse pas un humoriste), one can place it to the credit of Longfellow that he had already won for himself some sort of literary standing in the presence of one Frenchman. At the time of this complaint, it may be noticed that Mr. S. L. Clemens was a boy of fifteen. The usual European criticism at the present day is not that America produces so few humorists, but that she brings forth so many.

The work which came next from Longfellow's pen has that peculiar value to a biographer which comes from a distinct, unequivocal, low-water mark in the intellectual product with which he has to deal. This book, "Kavanagh," had the curious fate of bringing great disappointment to most of his friends and admirers, and yet of being praised by the two among his contemporaries personally most successful in fiction, Hawthorne and Howells. Now that the New England village life has proved such rich material in the hands of Mary Wilkins, Sarah Jewett, and Rowland Robinson, it is difficult to revert to "Kavanagh" (1849) without feeling that it is from beginning to end a piece of purely academic literature without a type of character, or an incident--one might almost say without a single phrase--that gives quite the flavor of real life. Neither the joys nor the griefs really reach the reader's heart for one moment. All the characters use essentially the same dialect, and every sentence is duly supplied with its anecdote or illustration, each one of which is essentially bookish at last. It has been well said of it that it is an attempt to look at rural society as Jean Paul would have looked at it. Indeed, we find Longfellow reading aloud from the "Campaner Thal" while actually at work on "Kavanagh," and he calls the latter in his diary "a romance."{78} When we consider how remote Jean Paul seems from the present daily life of Germany, one feels the utter inappropriateness of his transplantation to New England. Yet Emerson read the book "with great contentment," and pronounced it "the best sketch we have seen in the direction of the American novel," and discloses at the end the real charm he found or fancied by attributing to it "elegance." Hawthorne, warm with early friendship, pronounces it "a most precious and rare book, as fragrant as a bunch of flowers and as simple as one flower.... Nobody but yourself would dare to write so quiet a book, nor could any other succeed in it. It is entirely original, a book by itself, a true work of genius, if ever there was one." Nothing, I think, so well shows us the true limitations of American literature at that period as these curious phrases. It is fair also to recognize that Mr. W. D. Howells, writing nearly twenty years later, says with almost equal exuberance, speaking of "Kavanagh," "It seems to us as yet quite unapproached by the multitude of New England romances that have followed it in a certain delicate truthfulness, as it is likely to remain unsurpassed in its light humor and pensive grace."{79}

The period following the publication of "Evangeline" seemed a more indeterminate and unsettled time than was usual with Longfellow. He began a dramatic romance of the age of Louis XIV., but did not persist in it, and apart from the story of "Kavanagh" did no extended work. He continued to publish scattered poems, and in two years (1850) there appeared another volume called "The Seaside and the Fireside" in which the longest contribution and the most finished--perhaps the most complete and artistic which he ever wrote--was called "The Building of the Ship." To those who remember the unequalled voice and dramatic power of Mrs. Kemble, it is easy to imagine the enthusiasm with which her reading of this poem was received by an audience of three thousand, and none the less because at that troubled time the concluding appeal to the Union had a distinct bearing on the conflicts of the time. For the rest of the volume, it included the strong and lyric verses called "Seaweed," which were at the time criticised by many, though unreasonably, as rugged and boisterous; another poem of dramatic power, "Sir Humphrey Gilbert;" and one of the most delicately imaginative and musical among all he ever wrote, "The Fire of Drift-Wood," the scene of which was the Devereux Farm at Marblehead. There were touching poems of the fireside, especially that entitled "Resignation," written in 1848 after the death of his little daughter Fanny, and one called "The Open Window." Looking back from this, his fourth volume of short poems, it must be owned that he had singularly succeeded in providing against any diminution of power or real monotony. Nevertheless his next effort was destined to be on a wider scale.

{74 Mistakenly described by the Rev. Samuel Longfellow as "nearly four hundred pages." Life, ii. 3.}

{75 Life, iii. 370.}

{76 Life, iii. 94.}

{77 Correspondence of R. W. Griswold, p. 162.}

{78 Life, ii. 81.}

{79 North American Review, civ. 534.}

CHAPTER XVII

RESIGNATION OF PROFESSORSHIP--TO DEATH OF MRS. LONGFELLOW

On the last day of 1853, Longfellow wrote in his diary, "How barren of all poetic production and even prose production this last year has been! For 1853 I have absolutely nothing to show. Really there has been nothing but the college work. The family absorbs half the time, and letters and visits take out a huge cantle." Yet four days later he wrote, January 4, 1854, "Another day absorbed in the college. But why complain? These golden days are driven like nails into the fabric. Who knows but they help it to hold fast and firm?" On February 22, he writes, "You are not misinformed about my leaving the professorship. I am 'pawing to get free.'" On his birthday, February 27, he writes, in the joy of approaching freedom, "I am curious to know what poetic victories, if any, will be won this year." On April 19 he writes, "At eleven o'clock in No. 6 University Hall, I delivered my last lecture--the last I shall ever deliver, here or anywhere."{80} The following are the letters explaining this, and hitherto unpublished, but preserved in the Harvard College archives.

CAMBRIDGE, February 16, 1854.

GENTLEMEN,--In pursuance of conversations held with Dr. Walker, the subject of which he has already communicated to you,--I now beg leave to tender you my resignation of the "Smith Professorship of the French and Spanish Languages and Literatures," which I have held in Harvard College since the year 1835.

Should it be in your power to appoint my successor before the beginning of the next Term, I should be glad to retire at once. But if this should be inconvenient, I will discharge the duties of the office until the end of the present Academic Year.

I venture on this occasion, Gentlemen, to call your attention to the subject of the salaries paid to the several Instructors in this Department, and to urge, as far as may be proper, such increase as may correspond to the increased expenses of living in this part of the country at the present time.

With sentiments of the highest regard, and sincere acknowledgments of your constant courtesy and kindness, during the eighteen years of my connection with the College,

I have the honor to be, Gentlemen, Your Obt. Servt.

HENRY W. LONGFELLOW.{81}

To the President and Corporation of Harvard University.

[TO PRESIDENT WALKER.]

CAMBRIDGE, Feb. 16, 1854.

MY DEAR SIR,--I inclose you my note to the Corporation. Will you be kind enough to look at it, before handing it to them; for if it is not in proper form and phrase, I will write it over again.

I also inclose the letters of Schele de Vere, and remain,

Very faithfully Yours

HENRY W. LONGFELLOW{82}

P. S. I have not assigned any reasons for my resignation, thinking it better to avoid a repetition of details, which I have already explained to you.

[TO THE PRESIDENT AND FELLOWS OF HARVARD COLLEGE.]

GENTLEMEN,--Having last Winter signified to you my intention of resigning my Professorship at the close of the present College year, I now beg leave to tender you my resignation more formally and officially.

It is eighteen years since I entered upon the duties of this Professorship. They have been to me pleasant and congenial; and I hope I have discharged them to your satisfaction, and to the advantage of the College in whose prosperity I shall always take the deepest interest.

In dissolving a connection, which has lasted so long, and which has been to me a source of so much pleasure and advantage, permit me to express to you my grateful thanks for the confidence you have reposed in me, and the many marks of kindness and consideration which I have received at your hands.

With best wishes for the College and for yourselves, I have the honor to be, Gentlemen,

Your Obedient Servant

HENRY W. LONGFELLOW

Smith Professor of French and Spanish, and Professor of Belles Lettres.{83}

CAMBRIDGE, August 23, 1854.

[TO PRESIDENT WALKER.]

NAHANT, Aug. 23, 1854.

MY DEAR SIR,--I inclose you the Letter of resignation we were speaking of yesterday. I have made it short, as better suited to College Records; and have said nothing of the regret, which I naturally feel on leaving you, for it hardly seems to me that I am leaving you; and little of my grateful acknowledgments; for these I hope always to show, by remaining the faithful friend and ally of the College.

I beg you to make my official farewells to the members of the Faculty at their next meeting, and to assure them all and each of my regard and friendship, and of my best wishes for them in all things.

With sentiments of highest esteem, I remain

Dear Sir, Yours faithfully

HENRY W. LONGFELLOW{84}

His retirement was not a matter of ill health, for he was perfectly well, except that he could not use his eyes by candle-light. But friends and guests and children and college lectures had more and more filled up his time, so that he had no strength for poetry, and the last two years had been very unproductive. There was, moreover, all the excitement of his friend Sumner's career, and of the fugitive slave cases in Boston, and it is no wonder that he writes in his diary, with his usual guarded moderation, "I am not, however, very sure as to the result." Meanwhile he sat for his portrait by Lawrence, and the subject of the fugitive slave cases brought to the poet's face, as the artist testified, a look of animation and indignation which he was glad to catch and retain. On Commencement Day, July 19, 1854, he wore his academical robes for the last time, and writes of that event, "The whole crowded church looked ghostly and unreal as a thing in which I had no part." He had already been engaged upon his version of Dante, having taken it up on February 1, 1853,{85} after ten years' interval; and moreover another new literary project had occurred to him "purely in the realm of fancy," as he describes it, and his freedom became a source of joy.

He had been anxious for some years to carry out his early plan of works upon American themes. He had, as will be remembered, made himself spokesman for the Indians on the college platform. His list of proposed subjects had included as far back as 1829, "Tales of the Quoddy Indians," with a description of Sacobezon, their chief. After twenty-five years he wrote in his diary (June 22, 1854), "I have at length hit upon a plan for a poem on the American Indians which seems to be the right one and the only. It is to weave together their beautiful traditions into a whole. I have hit upon a measure, too, which I think the right one and the only one for the purpose." He had to draw for this delineation not merely upon the Indians seen in books, but on those he had himself observed in Maine, the Sacs and Foxes he had watched on Boston Common, and an Ojibway chief whom he had entertained at his house. As for the poetic measure, a suitable one had just been suggested to him by the Finnish epic of "Kalevala," which he had been reading; and he had been delighted by its appropriateness to the stage character to be dealt with and the type of legend to be treated. "Hiawatha" was begun on June 25, 1854, and published on November 10 of that year. He enjoyed the work thoroughly, but it evidently seemed to him somewhat tame before he got through, and this tendency to tameness was sometimes a subject of criticism with readers; but its very simplicity made the style attractive to children and gave a charm which it is likely always to retain. With his usual frankness, he stated at the outset that the metre was not original with him, and it was of course a merit in the legends that they were not original. The book received every form of attention; it was admired, laughed at, parodied, set to music, and publicly read, and his fame unquestionably rests far more securely on this and other strictly American poems than on the prolonged labor of the "Golden Legend." He himself writes that some of the newspapers are "fierce and furious" about "Hiawatha," and again "there is the greatest pother over 'Hiawatha.'" Freiligrath, who translated the poem into German, writes him from London, "Are you not chuckling over the war which is waging in the 'Athenem' about the measure from 'Hiawatha'?" He had letters of hearty approval from Emerson, Hawthorne, Parsons, and Bayard Taylor; the latter, perhaps, making the best single encomium on the book in writing to its author, "The whole poem floats in an atmosphere of the American 'Indian summer.'" The best tribute ever paid to it, however, was the actual representation of it as a drama by the Ojibway Indians on an island in Lake Huron, in August, 1901, in honor of a visit to the tribe by some of the children and grandchildren of the poet. This posthumous tribute to a work of genius is in itself so picturesque and interesting and has been so well described by Miss Alice Longfellow, who was present, that I have obtained her consent to reprint it in the Appendix to this volume.

Longfellow's next poem reverted to hexameters once more, inasmuch as "Evangeline" had thoroughly outlived the early criticisms inspired by this meter. The theme had crossed his mind in 1856, and he had begun to treat it in dramatic form and verse, under the name it now bears; but after a year's delay he tried it again under the name of Priscilla, taking the name, possibly, from an attractive English Quakeress, Priscilla Green, whose sweet voice had charmed him in a public meeting, "breaking now and then," as he says, "into a kind of rhythmic charm in which the voice seemed floating up and down on wings." It has been thought that he transferred in some degree the personality of this worthy woman to the heroine of his story, their Christian names being the same; but he afterwards resumed the original title, "The Courtship of Miles Standish." He wrote it with great ease between December, 1857, and March, 1858, and perhaps never composed anything with a lighter touch or more unmingled pleasure. Twenty-five thousand copies were sold or ordered of the publishers during the first week, and ten thousand in London on the first day. In both theme and treatment the story was thoroughly to his liking, and vindicated yet further that early instinct which guided him to American subjects. Longfellow was himself descended, it will be remembered, from the very marriage he described, thus guaranteeing a sympathetic treatment, while the measure is a shade crisper and more elastic than that of "Evangeline," owing largely to the greater use of trochees. It is almost needless to say that no such effort can ever be held strictly to the classic rules, owing to the difference in the character of the language. With German hexameters the analogy is closer.

On July 10, 1861, Mrs. Longfellow died the tragic death which has been so often described, from injuries received by fire the day before. Never was there a greater tragedy within a household; never one more simply and nobly borne. It was true to Lowell's temperament to write frankly his sorrow in exquisite verse; but it became Longfellow's habit, more and more, to withhold his profoundest feelings from spoken or written utterance; and it was only after his death that his portfolio, being opened, revealed this sonnet, suggested by a picture of the western mountain whose breast bears the crossed furrows.

THE CROSS OF SNOW

In the long, sleepless watches of the night, A gentle face--the face of one long dead-- Looks at me from the wall, where round its head The night-lamp casts a halo of pale light. Here in this room she died; and soul more white Never through martyrdom of fire was led To its repose; nor can in books be read The legend of a life more benedight. There is a mountain in the distant West That, sun-defying, in its deep ravines Displays a cross of snow upon its side. Such is the cross I wear upon my breast These eighteen years, through all the changing scenes And seasons, changeless since the day she died.

July 10, 1879.

{80 Life, ii. 262, 263, 265, 266, 268.}

{81 Harvard College Papers [MS.], 2d ser. xx. 345.}

{82 Ib. 347.}

{83 Harvard College Papers [MS.], 2d ser. xxi. 249.}

{84 Harvard College Papers [MS.], 2d ser. xxi. 249.}

{85 Life, ii. 248.}

CHAPTER XVIII

BIRDS OF PASSAGE

Longfellow had always a ready faculty for grouping his shorter poems in volumes, and had a series continuing indefinitely under the name of "Birds of Passage," which in successive "flights" were combined with longer works. The first was contained in the volume called "The Courtship of Miles Standish" (1858); the second in "Tales of a Wayside Inn" (1863); flight the third appeared in connection with "Aftermath" (1873); flight the fourth in "Masque of Pandora and Other Poems" (1875), and flight the fifth in "Keramos and Other Poems" (1878). These short poems stand representative of his middle life, as "Voices of the Night" and "Ballads" did for the earlier; and while the maturer works have not, as a whole, the fervor and freshness of the first, they have more average skill of execution.

The "Tales of a Wayside Inn" was the final grouping of several stories which had accumulated upon him, large and small, and finally demanded a title-page in common. Some of them had been published before and were grouped into a volume in 1863, which, making itself popular, was followed by two more volumes, finally united into one. We have what is not usually the case, the poet's own account of them, he having written thus to a correspondent in England: "'The Wayside Inn' has more foundation in fact than you may suppose. The town of Sudbury is about twenty miles from Cambridge. Some two hundred years ago, an English family by the name of Howe built there a country house, which has remained in the family down to the present time, the last of the race dying but two years ago. Losing their fortune, they became innkeepers; and for a century the Red-Horse Inn has flourished, going down from father to son. The place is just as I have described it, though no longer an inn. All this will account for the landlord's coat-of-arms, and his being a justice of the peace, and his being known as 'the Squire,'--things that must sound strange in English ears. All the characters are real. The musician is Ole Bull; the Spanish Jew, Israel Edrehi, whom I have seen as I have painted him," etc., etc.

Other participants in the imaginary festivities are the late Thomas W. Parsons, the translator of Dante, who appears as the poet; the theologian being Professor Daniel Treadwell of Harvard University, an eminent physicist, reputed in his day to be not merely a free thinker, but something beyond it; the student being Henry Ware Wales, a promising scholar and lover of books, who left his beautiful library to the Harvard College collection; and the Sicilian being Luigi Monti, who had been an instructor in Italian at Harvard under Longfellow. Several of this group had habitually spent their summers in the actual inn which Longfellow described and which is still visible at Sudbury. But none of the participants in the supposed group are now living except Signor Monti, who still resides in Rome, as for many years back, with his American wife, a sister of the poet Parsons. All the members of the group were well known in Cambridge and Boston, especially Ole Bull, who was at seventy as picturesque in presence and bearing as any youthful troubadour, and whose American wife, an active and courageous philanthropist, still vibrates between America and India, and is more or less allied to the Longfellow family by the marriage of her younger brother, Mr. J. G. Thorp, to the poet's youngest daughter. The volume has always been popular, even its most ample form; yet most of the individual poems are rarely quoted, and with the exception of "Paul Revere's Ride" and "Lady Wentworth" they are not very widely read. These two are, it is to be observed, the most essentially American among them. The book was originally to have been called "The Sudbury Tales," and was sent to the printer in April, 1863, under that title, which was however changed to "Tales of a Wayside Inn," through the urgency of Charles Sumner.

It is the common fate of those poets who live to old age, that their critics, or at least their contemporary critics, are apt to find their later work less valuable than their earlier. Browning, Tennyson, and Swinburne, to mention no others, have had to meet this fate, and Longfellow did not escape it. Whether it is that the fame of the earlier work goes on accumulating while the later has not yet been tested by time, or that contemporary admirers have grown older and more critical when they are introduced to the later verses, this is hard to decide. Even when the greatest of modern poets completed in old age the dream of his youth, it was the fashion for a long time to regard the completion as a failure, and it took years to secure any real appreciation to the second part of "Faust." This possibility must always be allowed for, but the fact remains that the title which Longfellow himself chose for so many of his poems, "Birds of Passage," was almost painfully suggestive of a series of minor works of which we can only say that had his fame rested on those alone, it would have been of quite uncertain tenure. A very few of them, like "Keramos," "Morituri Salutamus," and "The Herons of Elmwood," stand out as exceptions, and above all of these was the exquisite sonnet already printed in this volume, "The Cross of Snow," recording at last the poet's high water-mark, as was the case with Tennyson's "Crossing the Bar." Apart from these, it may be truly said that the little volume called "Flower de Luce" was the last collection published by him which recalled his earlier strains. His volume "Ultima Thule" appeared in 1880, and "In the Harbor," classed as a second part to it, but issued by others after his death. With these might be placed, though not with any precision, the brief tragedy of "Judas Maccabas," which had been published in the "Three Books of Song," in 1872; and the unfinished fragment, "Michael Angelo," which was found in his desk after death. None of his dramatic poems showed him to be on firm ground in respect to this department of poesy, nor can they, except the "Golden Legend," be regarded as altogether successful literary undertakings. It is obvious that historic periods differ wholly in this respect; and all we can say is that while quite mediocre poets were good dramatists in the Elizabethan period, yet good poets have usually failed as dramatists in later days. Longfellow's efforts on this very ground were not less successful, on the whole, than those of Tennyson and Swinburne; nor does even Browning, tried by the test of the actual stage, furnish a complete exception.

CHAPTER XIX

LAST TRIP TO EUROPE

On May 27, 1868, Longfellow sailed from New York for Liverpool in the steamer Russia, with a large family party, including his son and his son's bride, his three young daughters, his brother and two sisters, with also a brother-in-law, the brilliant Thomas G. Appleton. On arrival they went at once to the English lakes, visiting Furness Abbey, Corby Castle, and Eden Hall, where he saw still unimpaired the traditional goblet which Uhland's ballad had vainly attempted to shatter. At Morton, near Carlisle, while staying with a friend he received a public address, to which he thus replied, in one of the few speeches of his life:--

"MR. PRESIDENT AND GENTLEMEN,--Being more accustomed to speak with the pen than with the tongue, it is somewhat difficult for me to find appropriate words now to thank you for the honor you have done me, and the very kind expressions you have used. Coming here as a stranger, this welcome makes me feel that I am not a stranger; for how can a man be a stranger in a country where he finds all doors and all hearts open to him? Besides, I myself am a Cumberland man,--I was born in the County of Cumberland, in the State of Maine, three thousand miles from here,--and you all know that the familiar name of a town or country has a homelike sound to our ears.... You can think then how very grateful it is to me--how very pleasant--to find my name has a place in your memories and your affections. For this kindness I most heartily thank you, and I reciprocate all the good wishes which you have expressed for perpetual peace and amity between our two nations."{86}

He received the honorary degree of Doctor of Laws at Cambridge, and the scene was thus described by a London reporter:--

"Amid a score or so of Heads of Houses and other Academic dignitaries conspicuous by their scarlet robes, the one on whom all eyes were turned was Henry Wadsworth Longfellow. The face was one which would have caught the spectator's glance, even if not called to it by the cheers which greeted his appearance in the red robes of an LL. D. Long, white, silken hair and a beard of patriarchal whiteness enclosed a fresh-colored countenance, with fine-cut features and deep-sunken eyes, overshadowed by massive eyebrows. In a few well-rounded Latin sentences, Mr. Clark, the Public Orator, recited the claims of the distinguished visitor to the privilege of an honorary degree. The names of Hiawatha and Evangeline sounded strangely amid the sonorous periods."{87}

Another journalist wrote that the orator "drew a picture of the function of poetry to solace the ills of life and draw men from its low cares ad excelsiora. This point was caught at once by the undergraduates and drew forth hearty cheering. The degree was then conferred."{88}

Arriving in London he received a deluge of cards and invitations; visited Windsor by invitation of the Queen, and was received in one of the galleries of the castle; called by request upon the Prince of Wales; and was entertained at dinner by Mr. Bierstadt, the landscape painter, who had several hundred people to meet him. Mr. Longfellow had stipulated that there should be no speeches, but after dinner there were loud calls for Mr. Gladstone, who said in reply, according to the reporters, that "they must be permitted to break through the restrictions which the authority of their respected host had imposed upon them, and to give expression to the feelings which one and all entertained on this occasion. After all, it was simply impossible to sit at the social board with a man of Mr. Longfellow's world-wide fame, without offering him some tribute of their admiration. There was perhaps no class of persons less fitted to do justice to an occasion of this character than those who were destined to tread the toilsome and dusty road of politics. Nevertheless, he was glad to render his tribute of hearty admiration to one whom they were glad to welcome not only as a poet but as a citizen of America."{89}

Mr. Longfellow replied that "they had taken him by surprise, a traveller just landed and with Bradshaw still undigested upon his brain, and they would not expect him to make a speech. There were times, indeed, when it was easier to speak than to act; but it was not so with him, now. He would, however, be strangely constituted if he did not in his heart respond to their kind and generous welcome. In the longest speech he could make, he could but say in many phrases what he now said in a few sincere words,--that he was deeply grateful for the kindness which had been shown him."{90}

After visiting the House of Lords with Mr. R. C. Winthrop, on one occasion, he was accosted by a laboring man in the street, who asked permission to speak with him, and recited a verse of "Excelsior," before which the poet promptly retreated. Passing to the continent, the party visited Switzerland, crossed by the St. Gothard Pass to Italy, and reached Cadenabbia, on the Lake of Como. They returned to Paris in the autumn; then went to Italy again, staying at Florence and Rome, where they saw the Abb?Liszt and obtained that charming sketch of him by Healy, in which the great musician is seen opening the inner door and bearing a candle in his hand. In the spring they visited Naples, Venice, and Innsbruck, returning then to England, where Longfellow received the degree of D. C. L. at Oxford; and they then visited Devonshire, Edinburgh, and the Scottish lakes. He again received numberless invitations in London, and wrote to Lowell, "It is only by dint of great resolution that I escaped a dozen public and semi-public dinners." At the very last moment before sailing, he received a note from Mr. E. J. Reed, the chief constructor to the British Navy, who pronounced his poem "The Building of the Ship" to be the finest poem on shipbuilding that ever was or ever would be written. He reached home September 1, 1869. In his letters during this period, one sees the serene head of a family, the absolutely unspoiled recipient of praise, but not now the eager and enthusiastic young pilgrim of romance. Yet he writes to his friend Ferguson that if he "said his say" about York Cathedral, his friends would think him sixteen instead of sixty; and again tells his publisher Fields that he enjoys Lugano--never before visited--to the utmost, but that "the old familiar place saddened" him.{91} Many a traveller has had in later life the same experience.

{86 Life, iii. 111.}

{87 Life, iii. 111, 112.}

{88 Ib. 112.}

{89 Life, iii. 114.}

{90 Ib. 114, 115.}

{91 Life, iii. 122.}

CHAPTER XX

DANTE

We come now to that great task which Longfellow, after an early experiment, had dropped for years, and which he resumed after his wife's death, largely for the sake of an absorbing occupation. Eighteen years before, November 24, 1843, he had written to Ferdinand Freiligrath that he had translated sixteen cantos of Dante, and there seems no reason to suppose that he had done aught farther in that direction until this new crisis. After resuming the work, he translated for a time a canto as each day's task, and refers to this habit in his sonnet on the subject, where he says:--

"I enter here from day to day, And leave my burden at this minster gate."

The work was not fully completed until 1866, and was published in part during the following year.

The whole picture of the manner in which the work was done has long been familiar to the literary world, including the pleasing glimpse of the little circle of cultivated friends, assembled evening after evening, to compare notes and suggest improvements. For many years this was regarded by students and critics as having been almost an ideal method for the production of a great work, and especially of a translation,--a task where there is always the original text at hand for reference. As time has gone on, however, the admiration for the completed work has gradually been mingled with a growing doubt whether this species of joint production was on the whole an ideal one, and whether, in fact, a less perfect work coming from a single mind might not surpass in freshness of quality, and therefore in successful effort, any joint product. Longfellow had written long before to Freiligrath that making a translation was "like running a ploughshare through the soil of one's mind,"{92} and it would be plainly impossible to run ploughshares simultaneously through half a dozen different minds at precisely the same angle. The mind to decide on a phrase or an epithet, even in a translation, must, it would seem, be the mind from which the phrase or statement originally proceeded; a suggestion from a neighbor might sometimes be most felicitous, but quite as often more tame and guarded; and the influence of several neighbors collectively might lie, as often happens in the outcome of an ordinary committee meeting, rather in the direction of caution than of vigor. Longfellow's own temperament was of the gracious and conciliatory type, by no means of the domineering quality; and it is certainly a noticeable outcome of all this joint effort at constructing a version of this great world-poem, that one of the two original delegates, Professor Norton, should ultimately have published a prose translation of his own. It is also to be observed that Professor Norton, in the original preface to his version, while praising several other translators, does not so much as mention the name of Longfellow; and in his list of "Aids to the Study of the 'Divine Comedy'" speaks only of Longfellow's notes and illustrations, which he praises as "admirable." Even Lowell, the other original member of the conference, while in his "Dante" essay he ranks Longfellow's as "the best" of the complete translations, applies the word "admirable" only to those fragmentary early versions, made for Longfellow's college classes twenty years before,--versions which the completed work was apparently intended to supersede.

Far be it from me to imply that any disloyalty was shown on the part of these gentlemen either towards their eminent associate or towards the work on which they had shared his labors; it is only that they surprise us a little by what they do not say. It may be that they do not praise the Longfellow version because they confessedly had a share in it, yet this reason does not quite satisfy. Nothing has been more noticeable in the popular reception of the completed work than the general preference of unsophisticated readers for those earlier translations thus heartily praised by Lowell. There has been a general complaint that the later work does not possess for the English-speaking reader the charm exerted by the original over all who can read Italian, while those earlier and fragmentary specimens had certainly possessed something of that charm.

Those favorite versions, it must be remembered, were not the result of any cooperated labor, having been written by Professor Longfellow in an interleaved copy of Dante which he used in the class room. They were three in number, all from the "Purgatorio" and entitled by him respectively, "The Celestial Pilot," "The Terrestrial Paradise," and "Beatrice." They were first published in "Voices of the Night" (1839), and twenty-eight years had passed before the later versions appeared. Those twenty-eight years had undoubtedly enhanced in width and depth Mr. Longfellow's knowledge of the Italian language; their labors and sorrows had matured the strength of his mind; but it is not so clear that they had not in some degree diminished its freshness and vivacity, nor is it clear that the council of friendly critics would be an influence tending to replace just those gifts.

If a comparison is to be made between the earlier and later renderings, the best way would doubtless be to place them side by side in parallel columns; and while it would be inappropriate to present such a comparison here on any large scale, it may be worth while to take a passage at random to see the effect of the two methods. Let us take, for instance, a passage from "Purgatorio," canto xxx. lines 22 and 23. They are thus in the original:--

"Io vidi gi?nel cominciar del giorno La parte oriental tutta rosata, E l'altro ciel di bel sereno adorno."

The following is Longfellow's translation of 1839, made by the man of thirty-two:--

"Oft have I seen, at the approach of day, The orient sky all stained with roseate hues, And the other heaven with light serene adorned."

The following is the later version, made by the man of sixty, after ample conference with friendly critics:--

"Ere now have I beheld, as day began, The eastern hemisphere all tinged with rose, And the other heaven with fair serene adorned;"

I do not see how any English-speaking reader could hesitate for a moment in finding a charm far greater in the first version than in the second, or fail to recognize in it more of that quality which has made the name of Dante immortal. If this be true, the only question that can be raised is whether this advantage has been won by a sacrifice of that degree of literalness which may fairly be demanded of a translation in poetic form. Perfect and absolute literalness, it must be remembered, can only be expected of a prose version, and even after the most perfect metrical translation a prose version may be as needful as ever. Let us consider for a moment the two examples as given above. It may be conceded at the outset that the adverb gi?is more strictly and carefully rendered by "ere" than by "oft," but the difference is not important, as any one old enough to describe a daybreak has undoubtedly seen more than one. The difference between "the approach of day" and "as day began" is important, since the last moment of the approach coincides with the first moment of the beginning. In the second line, "la parte oriental" is both more literally and more tersely rendered by "the orient sky," than by the more awkward expression "the eastern hemisphere," unless it be claimed that "sky" does not sufficiently recognize the earth as seen in the view; to which it may justly be replied that the word "hemisphere," if applied only to the earth, equally omits the sky, and the two defects balance each other. "Tinged with rose" is undoubtedly a briefer expression for the untranslatable "rosata" than "stained with roseate hues" would be. The last line of the three finds an identical rendering in the two versions, and while "bel sereno" is more literally rendered by "fair serene" than by "light serene," yet the earlier phrase has the advantage of being better English, serene being there used as an adjective only, whereas in the later translation it is used as a noun, a practice generally regarded as obsolete in the dictionaries. Even where the word is thus employed, they tell us, it does not describe the morning light, but indicates, like the French word "serein," an evening dampness; as where Daniel says, "The fogs and the serene offend us." Summing up the comparison, so far as this one example goes, it would seem that the revised version of Longfellow has but very slight advantage over its predecessor, while the loss of vividness and charm is unquestionable.

To carry the test yet farther, let us compare the three lines, in their two successive versions, with the prose version of Professor Norton, which reads as follows: "I have seen ere now at the beginning of the day the eastern region all rosy, while the rest of heaven was beautiful with fair, clear sky." Here the prose translator rightly discards the "oft" of the earlier Longfellow version, but his "at the beginning" is surely nearer to the "at the approach" of the first version than to the less literal "as day began" of the second. The prose "the eastern region" conforms to the second version "the eastern hemisphere," but surely the Italian "la parte oriental" is more nearly met by "the orient sky" than by either of these heavier and more geographical substitutes, which have a flavor of the text-book. Both the Longfellow versions have "the other heaven," which is a literal rendering of "l'altro ciel," whereas "the rest of heaven" is a shade looser in expression, and "fair, clear sky" also forfeits the condensation of "light serene" or "fair serene," of which two phrases the first seems the better, for reasons already given. On the whole, if we take Professor Norton's prose translation as the standard,

Longfellow's later version seems to me to gain scarcely anything upon the earlier in literalness, while it loses greatly in freshness and triumphant joyousness.

Nor is this in any respect an unreasonable criticism. For what does a translation exist, after all, if not to draw us toward that quality in the original which the translator, even at his best, can rarely reach? Goethe says that "the translator is a person who introduces you to a veiled beauty; he makes you long for the loveliness behind the veil," and we have in the notes to his "West-tliche Divan" the celebrated analysis of the three forms of translation. He there says, "Translation is of three kinds: First, the prosaic prose translation, which is useful in enriching the language of the translator with new ideas, but gives up all poetic art, and reduces even the poetic enthusiasm to one level watery plain. Secondly, the re-creation of the poem as a new poem, rejecting or altering all that seems foreign to the translator's nationality, producing a paraphrase which might, in the primal sense of the word, be called a parody. And, thirdly, ... the highest and last, where one strives to make the translation identical with the original; so that one is not instead of the other, but in the place of the other. This sort of translation ... 'approaches the interlinear version, and makes the understanding of the original a much easier task; thus we are led into the original,--yes, even driven in; and herein the great merit of this kind of translation lies.'"{93}

It may be doubted, however, whether Longfellow, in his remarkable paper "On the Translation of Faust" even if left to himself in making his version, could ever have reached the highest point attained by Goethe, from the mere difference between the two languages with which he and his original had to deal. The charm of Longfellow's earlier versions is, after all, an English charm, and perhaps the quality of Dante can no more be truthfully transmuted into this than we can transmute the charms of a spring morning into those of a summer afternoon, or violets into roses. Goethe, it is well known, took for his model as to the language of "Faust" the poetry of Hans Sachs, Longfellow's "cobbler bard;" and Dante's terse monosyllables were based upon the language of the people, which he first embodied in art. To mellow its refreshing brevities would perhaps be to destroy it, and that which Mr. Andrews finely says of the "Faust" may be still more true of the "Divina Commedia," that it "must remain, after all, the enchanted palace; and the bodies and the bones of those who in other days strove to pierce its encircling hedge lie scattered thickly about it." So Mr. W. C. Lawton, himself an experienced translator from the Greek, says of Longfellow's work, "His great version is but a partial success, for it essays the unattainable."{94} But if it be possible to win this success, it is probably destined to be done by one translator working singly and not in direct cooperation with others, however gifted or accomplished. Every great literary work needs criticism from other eyes during its progress. Nevertheless it will always remain doubtful whether any such work, even though it be a translation only, can be satisfactorily done by joint labor.

After all, when others have done their best, it is often necessary to fall back upon the French Joubert for the final touch of criticism; and in his unequalled formula for translating Homer, we find something not absolutely applicable to Dantean translation, yet furnishing much food for thought. The following is the passage: "There will never be an endurable translation of Homer, unless its words are chosen with skill and are full of variety, of freshness, and of charm. It is also essential that the diction should be as antique, as simple, as are the manners, the events, and the personages portrayed. With our modern style everything attitudinizes in Homer, and his heroes seem fantastic figures which personate the grave and proud."{95}

{92 Life, ii. 15.}

{93 I here follow the condensed version of Mr. W. P. Andrews, (Atlantic Monthly, lxvi., 733).}

{94 The New England Poets, p. 138.}

CHAPTER XXI

THE LOFTIER STRAIN: CHRISTUS

After all, no translation, even taken at its best, can wholly satisfy an essentially original mind. Longfellow wrote in his diary, November 19, 1849, as follows: "And now I long to try a loftier strain, the sublimer Song whose broken melodies have for so many years breathed through my soul in the better hours of life, and which I trust and believe will ere long unite themselves into a symphony not all unworthy the sublime theme, but furnishing 'some equivalent expression for the trouble and wrath of life, for its sorrow and its mystery.'"

This of course refers to the great poetic design of his life, "Christus, a Mystery," of which he wrote again on December 10, 1849, "A bleak and dismal day. Wrote in the morning 'The Challenge of Thor' as prologue or 'Introdus' to the second part of 'Christus.'" This he laid aside; just a month from that time he records in his diary, "In the evening, pondered and meditated the sundry scenes of 'Christus.'" Later, he wrote some half dozen scenes or more of "The Golden Legend" which is Part Second of "Christus," representing the medieval period. He afterwards wished, on reading Kingsley's "Saint's Tragedy," that he had chosen the theme of Elizabeth of Hungary in place of the minor one employed (Der Arme Heinrich), although if we are to judge by the comparative interest inspired by the two books, there is no reason for regret. At any rate his poem was published--the precursor by more than twenty years of any other portion of the trilogy of "Christus." The public, and even his friends, knew but little of his larger project, but "The Golden Legend" on its publication in 1851 showed more of the dramatic quality than anything else he had printed, and Ruskin gave to it the strong praise of saying, "Longfellow in his 'Golden Legend' has entered more closely into the temper of the monk, for good or for evil, than ever yet theological writer or historian, though they may have given their life's labor to the analysis."{96} It is to be noted that the passage in the book most criticised as unjust is taken from a sermon of an actual Italian preacher of the fifteenth century. But its accuracy or depth in this respect was probably less to the general public than its quality of readableness or that which G. P. R. James, the novelist, described as "its resemblance to an old ruin with the ivy and the rich blue mould upon it." If the rest of the long planned book could have been as successful as for the time being was the "Golden Legend," the dream of Longfellow's poetic life would have been fulfilled.

In view of such praise as Ruskin's, the question of anachronism more or less is of course quite secondary. Errors of a few centuries doubtless occur in it. Longfellow himself states the period at which he aims as 1230. But the spire of Strassburg Cathedral of which he speaks was not built until the fifteenth century, though the church was begun in the twelfth, when Walter the Minnesinger flourished. "The Lily of Medicine," which Prince Henry is reading when Lucifer drops in, was not written until after 1300, nor was St. John

Nepomuck canonized until after that date. The Algerine piracies did not begin until the sixteenth century. There were other such errors; yet these do not impair the merit of the book. Some curious modifications also appear in later editions. In the passage where the monk Felix is described in the first edition as pondering over a volume of St. Augustine, this saint disappears in later editions, while the Scriptures are substituted and the passage reads:--

"Wherein amazed he read A thousand years in thy sight Are but as yesterday when it is past And as a watch in the night;"

and in the next line "downcast" is substituted for "cast down," in order to preserve the rhyme. A very curious modification of a whole scene is to be found where the author ventured in the original edition (1851) to introduce a young girl at the midnight gaudiolum or carnival of the monks, she being apparently disguised as a monk, like Lucifer himself. This whole passage or series of passages was left out in the later editions, whether because it was considered too daring by his critics or perhaps not quite daring enough to give full spirit to the scene.

Turning now to "The New England Tragedies," we find that as far back as 1839, before he had conceived of "Christus," he had thought of a drama on Cotton Mather. Then a suggestion came to him in 1856 from his German friend, Emanuel Vitalis Scherb, of whom he writes on March 16, 1856: "Scherb wants me to write a poem on the Puritans and the Quakers. A good subject for a tragedy." On March 25 and 26 we find him looking over books on the subject, especially Besse's "Sufferings of the Quakers;" on April 2 he writes a scene of the play; on May 1 and 2 he is pondering and writing notes, and says: "It is delightful to revolve in one's mind a new conception." He also works upon it in a fragmentary way in July and in November, and remarks, in the midst of it, that he has lying on his table more than sixty requests for autographs. As a background to all of this lie the peculiar excitements of that stormy summer of 1856, when his friend Sumner was struck down in the United States Senate and he himself, meeting with an accident, was lamed for weeks and was unable to go to Europe with his children as he had intended. The first rough draft of "Wenlock Christison," whose title was afterwards changed to "John Endicott," and which was the first of "The New England Tragedies," was not finished till August 27, 1857, and the work alternated for a time with that done on "Miles Standish;" but it was more than ten years (October 10, 1868) before it was published, having first been written in prose, and only ten copies printed and afterwards rewritten in verse. With it was associated the second New England Tragedy, "Giles Corey" of the Salem farms, written rapidly in February of that same year. The volume never made a marked impression; even the sympathetic Mr. Fields, the publisher, receiving it rather coldly. It never satisfied even its author, and the new poetic idea which occurred to him on April 11, 1871, and which was to harmonize the discord of "The New England Tragedies" was destined never to be fulfilled. In the mean time, however, he carried them to Europe with him, and seems to have found their only admirer in John Forster, who wrote to him in London: "Your tragedies are very beautiful--beauty everywhere subduing and chastening the sadness; the pictures of nature in delightful contrast to the sorrowful and tragic violence of the laws; truth and unaffectedness everywhere. I hardly know which I like best; but there are things in 'Giles Corey' that have a strange attractiveness for me." Longfellow writes to Fields from Vevey, September 5, 1868: "I do not like your idea of calling the 'Tragedies' sketches. They are not sketches, and only seem so at first because I have studiously left out all that could impede the action. I have purposely made them simple and direct." He later adds: "As to anybody's 'adapting' these 'Tragedies' for the stage, I do not like the idea of it at all. Prevent this if possible. I should, however, like to have the opinion of some good actor--not a sensational actor--on that point. I should like to have Booth look at them." Six weeks later, having gone over to London to secure the copyright on these poems, he writes: "I saw also Bandmann, the tragedian, who expressed the liveliest interest in what I told him of the 'Tragedies.'" Finally he says, two days later, "Bandmann writes me a nice letter about the 'Tragedies,' but says they are not adapted to the stage. So we will say no more about that, for the present."{97}

"Christus: A Mystery" appeared as a whole in 1872, for the first time bringing together the three parts (I. "The Divine Tragedy;" II. "The Golden Legend," and III. "The New England Tragedies"). "The Divine Tragedy," which now formed the first part, was not only in some degree criticised as forming an anti-climax in being placed before the lighter portions of the great drama, but proved unacceptable among his friends, and was often subjected to the charge of being unimpressive and even uninteresting. On the other hand, we have the fact that it absorbed him more utterly than any other portion of the book. He writes in his diary on January 6, 1871, "The subject of 'The Divine

Tragedy' has taken entire possession of me, so that I can think of nothing else. All day pondering upon and arranging it." And he adds next day, "I find all hospitalities and social gatherings just now great interruptions." Yet he has to spend one morning that week in Boston at a meeting of stockholders; on another day Agassiz comes, broken down even to tears by the loss of health and strength; on another day there is "a continued series of interruptions from breakfast till dinner. I could not get half an hour to myself all day long. Oh, for a good snow-storm to block the door!" Still another day it is so cold he can scarcely write in his study, and he has "so many letters to answer." Yet he writes during that month a scene or two every day. We know from the experience of all poets that the most brilliant short poems may be achieved with wonderful quickness, but for a continuous and sustained effort an author surely needs some control over his own time.

It is a curious fact, never yet quite explained, that an author's favorite work is rarely that whose popular success best vindicates his confidence. This was perhaps never more manifest than in the case of Longfellow's "Christus" as a whole, and more especially that portion of it on which the author lavished his highest and most consecrated efforts, "The Divine Tragedy." Mr. Scudder has well said that "there is no one of Mr. Longfellow's writings which may be said to have so dominated his literary life" as the "Christus," and it shows his sensitive reticence that the portion of it which was first published, "The Golden Legend" (1851), gave to the reader no suggestion of its being, as we now know that it was, but a portion of a larger design. Various things came in the way, and before "The Divine Tragedy" appeared (1871) he had written of it, "I never had so many doubts and hesitations about any book as about this." On September 11 in that year he wrote in Nahant, "Begin to pack. I wish it were over and I in Cambridge. I am impatient to send 'The Divine Tragedy' to the printers." On the 18th of October he wrote: "The delays of printers are a great worry to authors;" on the 25th, "Get the last proof sheet of 'The Divine Tragedy;'" on the 30th, "Read over proofs of the 'Interludes' and 'Finale,' and am doubtful and perplexed;" on November 15, "All the last week, perplexed and busy with final correction of 'The Tragedy.'" It was published on December 12, and he writes to G. W. Greene, December 17, 1871, "'The Divine Tragedy' is very successful, from the booksellers' point of view--ten thousand copies were published on Tuesday last and the printers are already at work on three thousand more. That is pleasant, but that is not the main thing. The only question about a book ought to be whether it is successful in itself."

It is altogether probable that in the strict views then prevailing about the very letter of the Christian Scriptures, a certain antagonism may have prevailed, even toward the skill with which he transferred the sacred narratives into a dramatic form, just as it is found that among certain pious souls who for the first time yield their scruples so far as to enter a theatre, the mere lifting of the curtain seems to convey suggestions of sin. Be this as it may, we find in Longfellow's journal this brief entry (December 30): "Received from Routledge in London, three notices of 'The Tragedy,' all hostile." He, however, was cheered by the following letter from Horace Bushnell, then perhaps the most prominent among the American clergy for originality and spiritual freedom:--

HARTFORD, December 28, 1871.

DEAR SIR,--Since it will be a satisfaction to me to express my delight in the success of your poem, you cannot well deny me the privilege. When I heard the first announcement of it as forthcoming, I said, "Well, it is the grandest of all subjects; why has it never been attempted?" And yet I said inwardly in the next breath: "What mortal power is equal to the handling of it?" The greater and the more delightful is my surprise at the result. You have managed the theme with really wonderful address. The episodes, and the hard characters, and the partly imaginary characters, you had your liberty in; and you have used them well to suffuse and flavor and poetize the story. And yet, I know not how it is, but the part which finds me most perfectly, and is, in fact, the most poetic poetry of all, is the prose-poem,--the nearly rhythmic transcription of the simple narrative matter of the gospels. Perhaps the true account of it may be that the handling is so delicately reverent, intruding so little of the poet's fine thinking and things, that the reverence incorporate promotes the words and lifts the ranges of the sentiment; so that when the reader comes out at the close, he finds himself in a curiously new kind of inspiration, born of modesty and silence.

I can easily imagine that certain chaffy people may put their disrespect on you for what I consider your praise. Had you undertaken to build the Christ yourself, as they would require of you, I verily believe it would have killed you,--that is, made you a preacher.

With many thanks, I am yours,

HORACE BUSHNELL.{98}

It would not now be easy to ascertain what these hostile notices of "The Divine Tragedy" were, but it would seem that for some reason the poem did not, like its predecessors, find its way to the popular heart. When one considers the enthusiasm which greeted Willis' scriptural poems in earlier days, or that which has in later days been attracted by semi-scriptural prose fictions, such as "The Prince of the House of David" and "Ben Hur," the latter appearing, moreover, in a dramatic form, there certainly seems no reason why Longfellow's attempt to grapple with the great theme should be so little successful. The book is not, like "The New England Tragedies," which completed the circle of "Christus," dull in itself. It is, on the contrary, varied and readable; not merely poetic and tender, which was a matter of course in Longfellow's hands, but strikingly varied, its composition skilful, the scripture types well handled, and the additional figures, Helen of Tyre, Simon Magus, and Menahem the Essenian, skilfully introduced and effectively managed. Yet one rarely sees the book quoted; it has not been widely read, and in all the vast list of Longfellow translations into foreign languages, there appears no version of any part of it except the comparatively modern and medieval "Golden Legend." It has simply afforded one of the most remarkable instances in literary history of the utter ignoring of the supposed high watermark of a favorite author.

{96 Modern Painters, vol. v. chap. xx.}

{97 Life, iii. 123, 125.}

{98 Life, iii. 192, 193.}

CHAPTER XXII

WESTMINSTER ABBEY

Longfellow was the first American to be commemorated, on the mere ground of public service and distant kinship of blood, in Westminster Abbey.

The impressions made by that circumstance in America were very various, but might be classed under two leading attitudes. There were those to whom the English-speaking race seemed one, and Westminster Abbey its undoubted central shrine, an opinion of which Lowell was a high representative, as his speech on the occasion showed. There were those, on the other hand, to whom the American republic seemed a wholly new fact in the universe, and one which should have its own shrines. To this last class the "Hall of Fame," upon the banks of the Hudson, would appeal more strongly than Westminster Abbey; and it is probable that the interest inspired by that enterprise was partly due, at the outset, to the acceptance of Longfellow in England's greatest shrine. It may be fairly said, however, on reflection, that there is no absolute inconsistency between these two opinions. No one, surely, but must recognize the dignity of the proceeding when an American writer, born and bred, is, as it were, invited after death to stand as a permanent representative of his race in the storied abbey. On the other hand, it may easily be conceded that the dignitaries of Westminster are not, of themselves, necessarily so well versed in American claims as to make their verdict infallible or even approximate. The true solution would appear to be that in monuments, as in all other forms of recognition, each nation should have its own right of selection, and that it should be recognized as a gratifying circumstance when these independent judgments happen to coincide. The following is the best London report of the services on this occasion:--

"On Saturday, March 2, 1884, at midday, the ceremony of unveiling a bust of Longfellow took place in Poets' Corner, Westminster Abbey. It is the work of Mr. Thomas Brock, A. R. A., and was executed by desire of some five hundred admirers of the American poet. It stands on a bracket near the tomb of Chaucer, and between the memorials to Cowley and Dryden. Before the ceremony took place, a meeting of the subscribers was held in the Jerusalem Chamber. In the absence of Dean Bradley, owing to a death in his family, the Sub-Dean, Canon Prothero, was called to the chair.

"Mr. Bennoch having formally announced the order of proceeding, Dr. Bennett made a brief statement, and called upon Earl Granville to ask the Dean's acceptance of the bust.

"Earl Granville then said: 'Mr. Sub-Dean, Ladies and Gentlemen, ... I am afraid I cannot fulfil the promise made for me of making a speech on this occasion. Not that there are wanting materials for a speech; there are materials of the richest description. There are, first of all, the high character, the refinement, and the personal charm of the late illustrious poet,--if I may say so in the presence of those so near and so dear to him. There are also the characteristics of those works which have secured for him not a greater popularity in the United States themselves than in this island and in all the English-speaking dependencies of the British Empire. There are, besides, very large views with regard to the literature which is common to both the United States and ourselves, and with regard to the separate branches of literature which have sprung up in each country, and which act and react with so much advantage one upon another; and there are, above all, those relations of a moral and intellectual character which become bonds stronger and greater every day between the intellectual and cultivated classes of these two great countries. I am happy to say that with such materials there are persons here infinitely more fitted to deal than I could have been even if I had had time to bestow upon the thought and the labor necessary to condense into the limits of a speech some of the considerations I have mentioned. I am glad that among those present there is one who is not only the official representative of the United States, but who speaks with more authority than any one with regard to the literature and intellectual condition of that country. I cannot but say how glad I am that I have been present at two of the meetings held to inaugurate this work, and I am delighted to be present here to take part in the closing ceremony. With the greatest pleasure I make the offer of this memorial to the Sub-Dean; and from the kindness we have received already from the authorities of Westminster Abbey, I have no doubt it will be received in the same spirit. I beg to offer you, Mr. Sub-Dean, the bust which has been subscribed for.'

"The American Minister, Mr. Lowell, then said: 'Mr. Sub-Dean, my Lord, Ladies and Gentlemen, I think I may take upon myself the responsibility, in the name of the daughters of my beloved friend, to express their gratitude to Lord Granville for having found time, amid the continuous and arduous calls of his duty, to be present here this morning. Having occasion to speak in this place some two years ago, I remember that I then expressed the hope that some day or other the Abbey of Westminster would become the Valhalla of the whole English-speaking race. I little expected then that a beginning would be made so soon,--a beginning at once painful and gratifying in the highest degree to myself,--with the bust of my friend. Though there be no Academy in England which corresponds to that of France, yet admission to Westminster Abbey forms a sort of posthumous test of literary eminence perhaps as effectual. Every one of us has his own private Valhalla, and it is not apt to be populous. But the conditions of admission to the Abbey are very different. We ought no longer to ask why is so-and-so here, and we ought always to be able to answer the question why such a one is not here. I think that on this occasion I should express the united feeling of the whole English-speaking race in confirming the choice which has been made,--the choice of one whose name is dear to them all, who has inspired their lives and consoled their hearts, and who has been admitted to the fireside of all of them as a familiar friend. Nearly forty years ago I had occasion, in speaking of Mr. Longfellow, to suggest an analogy between him and the English poet Gray; and I have never since seen any reason to modify or change that opinion. There are certain very marked analogies between them, I think. In the first place, there is the same love of a certain subdued splendor, not inconsistent with transparency of diction; there is the same power of absorbing and assimilating the beauties of other literature without loss of originality; and, above all, there is that genius, that sympathy with universal sentiments and the power of expressing them so that they come home to everybody, both high and low, which characterize both poets. There is something also in that simplicity,--simplicity in itself being a distinction. But in style, simplicity and distinction must be combined in order to their proper effect; and the only warrant perhaps of permanence in literature is this distinction in style. It is something quite indefinable; it is something like the distinction of good-breeding, characterized perhaps more by the absence of certain negative qualities than by the presence of certain positive ones. But it seems to me that distinction of style is eminently found in the poet whom we are met here in some sense to celebrate to-day. This is not the place, of course, for criticism; still less is it the place for eulogy, for eulogy is but too often disguised apology. But I have been struck particularly--if I may bring forward one instance--with some of my late friend's sonnets, which seem to me to be some of the most beautiful and perfect we have in the language. His mind always moved straight towards its object, and was always permeated with the emotion that gave it frankness and sincerity, and at the same time the most ample expression. It seems that I should add a few words--in fact, I cannot refrain from adding a few words--with regard to the personal character of a man whom I knew for more than forty years, and whose friend I was honored to call myself for thirty years. Never was a private character more answerable to public performance than that of Longfellow. Never have I known a more beautiful character. I was familiar with it daily,--with the constant charity of his hand and of his mind. His nature was consecrated ground, into which no unclean spirit could ever enter. I feel entirely how inadequate anything that I can say is to the measure and proportion of an occasion like this. But I think I am authorized to accept, in the name of the people of America, this tribute to not the least distinguished of her sons, to a man who in every way, both in public and private, did honor to the country that gave him birth. I cannot add anything more to what was so well said in a few words by Lord Granville, for I do not think that these occasions are precisely the times for set discourses, but rather for a few words of feeling, of gratitude, and of appreciation.'

"The Sub-Dean, in accepting the bust, remarked that it was impossible not to feel, in doing so, that they were accepting a very great honor to the country. He could conceive that if the great poet were allowed to look down on the transactions of that day, he would not think it unsatisfactory that his memorial had been placed in that great Abbey among those of his brothers in poetry.

"The Chancellor of the Exchequer moved a vote of thanks to the honorary secretary and the honorary treasurer, and said he thought he had been selected for the duty because he had spent two or three years of his life in the United States, and a still longer time in some of the British colonies. It gave him the greater pleasure to do this, having known Mr. Longfellow in America, and having from boyhood enjoyed his poetry, which was quite as much appreciated in England and her dependencies as in America. Wherever he had been in America, and wherever he had met Americans, he had found there was one place at least which they looked upon as being as much theirs as it was England's--that place was the Abbey Church of Westminster. It seemed, therefore, to him that the present occasion was an excellent beginning of the recognition of the Abbey as what it had been called,--the Valhalla of the English-speaking people. He trusted this beginning would not be the end of its application in this respect.

"The company then proceeded to Poets' Corner, where, taking his stand in front of the covered bust,

"The Sub-Dean then said: 'I feel to-day that a double solemnity attaches to this occasion which calls us together. There is first the familiar fact that to-day we are adding another name to the great roll of illustrious men whom we commemorate within these walls, that we are adding something to that rich heritage which we have received of national glory from our ancestors, and which we feel bound to hand over to our successors, not only unimpaired, but even increased. There is then the novel and peculiar fact which attaches to the erection of a monument here to the memory of Henry Longfellow. In some sense, poets--great poets like him--may be said to be natives of all lands; but never before have the great men of other countries, however brilliant and widespread their fame, been admitted to a place in Westminster Abbey. A century ago America was just commencing her perilous path of independence and self-government. Who then could have ventured to predict that within the short space of one hundred years we in England should be found to honor an American as much as we could do so by giving his monument a place within the sacred shrine which holds the memories of our most illustrious sons? Is there not in this a very significant fact; is it not an emphatic proof of the oneness which belongs to our common race, and of the community of our national glories? May I not add, is it not a pledge that we give to each other that nothing can long and permanently sever nations which are bound together by the eternal ties of language, race, religion, and common feeling?'

"The reverend gentleman then removed the covering from the bust, and the ceremony ended."{99}

{99 Life, iii. 346-351.}

CHAPTER XXIII

LONGFELLOW AS A POET

The great literary lesson of Longfellow's life is to be found, after all, in this, that while he was the first among American poets to create for himself a world-wide fame, he was guided from youth to age by a strong national feeling, or at any rate by the desire to stand for the life and the associations by which he was actually surrounded. Such a tendency has been traced in this volume from his first childish poetry through his chosen theme for a college debate, his commencement oration, his plans formed during a first foreign trip, and the appeal made in his first really original paper in the "North American Review." All these elements of aim and doctrine were directly and explicitly American, and his most conspicuous poems, "Evangeline," "The Courtship of Miles Standish," "Hiawatha," and "The Wayside Inn," were unequivocally American also. In the group of poets to which he belonged, he was the most travelled and the most cultivated, in the ordinary sense, while Whittier was the least so; and yet they are, as we have seen, the two who--in the English-speaking world, at least--hold their own best; the line between them being drawn only where foreign languages are in question, and there Longfellow has of course the advantage. In neither case, it is to be observed, was this Americanism trivial, boastful, or ignoble in its tone. It would be idle to say that this alone constitutes, for an American, the basis of fame; for the high imaginative powers of Poe, with his especial gift of melody, though absolutely without national flavor, have achieved for him European fame, at least in France, this being due, however, mainly to his prose rather than to his poetry, and perhaps also the result, more largely than we recognize, of the assiduous discipleship of a single Frenchman, just as Carlyle's influence in America was due largely to Emerson. Be this as it may, it is certain that the hold of both Longfellow and Whittier is a thing absolutely due, first, to the elevated tone of their works, and secondly, that they have made themselves the poets of the people. No one can attend popular meetings in England without being struck with the readiness with which quotations from these two poets are heard from the lips of speakers, and this, while not affording the highest test of poetic art, still yields the highest secondary test, and one on which both these authors would doubtless have been willing to rest their final appeal for remembrance.

In looking back over Longfellow's whole career, it is certain that the early criticisms upon him, especially those of Margaret Fuller, had an immediate and temporary justification, but found ultimate refutation. The most commonplace man can be better comprehended at the end of his career than he can be analyzed at its beginning; and of men possessed of the poetic temperament, this is eminently true. We now know that at the very time when "Hyperion" and the "Voices of the Night" seemed largely European in their atmosphere, the author himself, in his diaries, was expressing that longing for American subjects which afterwards predominated in his career. Though the citizen among us best known in Europe, most sought after by foreign visitors, he yet gravitated naturally to American themes, American friends, home interests, plans, and improvements. He always voted at elections, and generally with the same party, took an interest in all local affairs and public improvements, headed subscription papers, was known by sight among children, and answered readily to their salutations. The same quality of citizenship was visible in his literary work. Lowell, who was regarded in England as an almost defiant American, yet had a distinct liking, which was not especially shared by Longfellow, for English ways. If people were ever misled on this point, which perhaps was not the case, it grew out of his unvarying hospitality and courtesy, and out of the fact vaguely recognized by all, but best stated by that keen critic, the late Mr. Horace E. Scudder, when he says of Longfellow: "He gave of himself freely to his intimate friends, but he dwelt, nevertheless, in a charmed circle, beyond the lines of which men could not penetrate.... It is rare that one in our time has been the centre of so much admiration, and still rarer that one has preserved in the midst of it all that integrity of nature which never abdicates."{100}

It is an obvious truth in regard to the literary works of Longfellow, that while they would have been of value at any time and place, their worth to a new and unformed literature was priceless. The first need of such a literature was no doubt a great original thinker, such as was afforded us in Emerson. But for him we should perhaps have been still provincial in thought and imitative in theme and illustration; our poets would have gone on writing about the skylark and the nightingale, which they might never have seen or heard anywhere, rather than about the bobolink and the humble-bee, which they knew. It was Emerson and the so-called Transcendentalists who really set our literature free; yet Longfellow rendered a service only secondary, in enriching and refining it and giving it a cosmopolitan culture, and an unquestioned standing in the literary courts of the civilized world. It was a great advantage, too, that in his more moderate and level standard of execution there was afforded no room for reaction. The same attributes that keep Longfellow from being the greatest of poets will make him also one of the most permanent. There will be no extreme ups and downs in his fame, as in that of those great poets of whom Ruskin writes, "Cast Coleridge at once aside, as sickly and useless; and Shelley as shallow and verbose." The finished excellence of his average execution will sustain it against that of profounder thinkers and more daring sons of song. His range of measures is not great, but his workmanship is perfect; he has always "the inimitable grace of not too much;" he has tested all literatures, all poetic motives, and all the simpler forms of versification, and he can never be taken unprepared. He will never be read for the profoundest stirring, or for the unlocking of the deepest mysteries; he will always be read for invigoration, for comfort, for content.

No man is always consistent, and it is not to be claimed that Longfellow was always ready to reaffirm his early attitude in respect to a national literature. It is not strange that after he had fairly begun to create one, he should sometimes be repelled by the class which has always existed who think that mere nationality should rank first and an artistic standard afterwards. He writes on July 24, 1844, to an unknown correspondent:--

"I dislike as much as any one can the tone of English criticism in reference to our literature. But when you say, 'It is a lamentable fact that as yet our country has taken no decided steps towards establishing a national literature,' it seems to me that you are repeating one of the most fallacious assertions of the English critics. Upon this point I differ entirely from you in opinion. A national literature is the expression of national character and thought; and as our character and modes of thought do not differ essentially from those of England, our literature cannot. Vast forests, lakes, and prairies cannot make great poets. They are but the scenery of the play, and have much less to do with the poetic character than has been imagined. Neither Mexico nor Switzerland has produced any remarkable poet.

"I do not think a 'Poets' Convention' would help the matter. In fact, the matter needs no helping."{101}

In the same way he speaks with regret, three years later, November 5, 1847, of "The prospectus of a new magazine in Philadelphia to build up 'a national literature worthy of the country of Niagara--of the land of forests and eagles.'"

One feels an inexhaustible curiosity as to the precise manner in which each favorite poem by a favorite author comes into existence. In the case of Longfellow we find this illustrated only here and there. We know that "The Arrow and the Song," for instance, came into his mind instantaneously; that "My Lost Youth" occurred to him in the night, after a day of pain, and was written the next morning; that on December 17, 1839, he read of shipwrecks reported in the papers and of bodies washed ashore near Gloucester, one lashed to a piece of the wreck, and that he wrote, "There is a reef called Norman's Woe where many of these took place; among others the schooner Hesperus. Also the Sea-Flower on Black Rock. I must write a ballad upon this; also two others,--'The Skeleton in Armor' and 'Sir Humphrey Gilbert.'" A fortnight later he sat at twelve o'clock by his fire, smoking, when suddenly it came into his mind to write the Ballad of the Schooner Hesperus, which he says, "I accordingly did. Then I went to bed, but could not sleep. New thoughts were running in my mind, and I got up to add them to the ballad. It was three by the clock. I then went to bed and fell asleep. I feel pleased with the ballad. It hardly cost me an effort. It did not come into my mind by lines, but by stanzas." A few weeks before, taking up a volume of Scott's "Border Minstrelsy," he had received in a similar way the suggestion of "The Beleaguered City" and of "The Luck of Edenhall."

We know by Longfellow's own statement to Mr. W. C. Lawton,{102} that it was his rule to do his best in polishing a poem before printing it, but afterwards to leave it untouched, on the principle that "the readers of a poem acquired a right to the poet's work in the form they had learned to love." He thought also that Bryant and Whittier hardly seemed happy in these belated revisions, and mentioned especially Bryant's "Water-Fowl,"

"As darkly limned upon the ethereal sky,"

where Longfellow preferred the original reading "painted on." It is, however, rare to find a poet who can carry out this principle of abstinence, at least in his own verse, and we know too surely that Longfellow was no exception; thus we learn that he had made important alterations in the "Golden Legend" within a few weeks of publication. These things show that his remark to Mr. Lawton does not tell quite the whole story. As with most poets, his alterations were not always improvements. Thus, in "The Wreck of the Hesperus," he made the fourth verse much more vigorous to the ear as it was originally written,--

"Then up and spoke an old sail Had sailed the Spanish Main,"

than when he made the latter line read

"Sailed to the Spanish Main,"

as in all recent editions. The explanation doubtless was that he at first supposed the "Spanish Main" to mean the Caribbean Sea; whereas it actually referred only to the southern shore of it. Still more curious is the history of a line in one of his favorite poems, "To a Child." Speaking of this, he says in his diary,{103} "Some years ago, writing an 'Ode to a Child,' I spoke of

'The buried treasures of the miser, Time.'

What was my astonishment to-day, in reading for the first time in my life Wordsworth's ode 'On the Power of Sound,' to read

'All treasures hoarded by the miser, Time.'"

As a matter of fact, this was not the original form of the Longfellow passage, which was,--

"The buried treasures of dead centuries,"

followed by

"The burning tropic skies."

More than this, the very word "miser" was not invariably used in this passage by the poet, as during an intermediate period it had been changed to "pirate," a phrase in some sense more appropriate and better satisfying the ear. The curious analogy to Wordsworth's line did not therefore lie in the original form of his own poem, but was an afterthought. It is fortunate that this curious combination of facts, all utterly unconscious on his part, did not attract the attention of Poe during his vindictive period.

It is to be noticed, however, that Longfellow apparently made all these changes to satisfy his own judgment, and did not make them, as Whittier and even Browning often did, in deference to the judgment of dull or incompetent critics. It is to be remembered that even the academic commentators on Longfellow still leave children to suppose that the Berserk's tale in "The Skeleton in Armor" refers to a supposed story that the Berserk was telling: although the word "tale" is unquestionably used in the sense of "tally" or "reckoning," to indicate how much ale the Norse hero could drink. Readers of Milton often misinterpret his line,

"And every shepherd tells his tale,"

in a similar manner, and the shepherd is supposed by many young readers to be pouring out a story of love or of adventure, whereas he is merely counting up the number of his sheep.

It will always remain uncertain how far Poe influenced the New England poets, whether by example or avoidance. That he sometimes touched Lowell, and not for good, is unquestionable, in respect to rhythm; but it will always remain a question whether his influence did not work in the other direction with Longfellow in making him limit himself more strictly to a narrow range of metrical structure. It was an admirable remark of Tennyson's that "every short poem should have a definite shape like the curve, sometimes a single, sometimes a double one, assumed by a severed tress, or the rind of an apple when flung to the floor."{104} This type of verse was rarely attempted by Longfellow, but he chose it most appropriately for "Seaweed" and in some degree succeeded. Poe himself in his waywardness could not adhere to it when he reached it, and after giving us in the original form of "Lenore," as published in "The Pioneer," perhaps the finest piece of lyric measure in our literature, made it over into a form of mere jingling and hackneyed rhythm, adding even the final commonplaceness of his tiresome "repetend." Lowell did something of the same in cutting down the original fine strain of the verses beginning "Pine in the distance," but Longfellow showed absolutely no trace of Poe, unless as a warning against multiplying such rhythmic experiments as he once tried successfully in "Seaweed." On the other hand, with all his love for Lowell, his native good taste kept him from the confused metaphors and occasional over-familiarities into which Lowell was sometimes tempted.

Perhaps the most penetrating remark made about Longfellow's art is that of Horace Scudder: "He was first of all a composer, and he saw his subjects in their relations, rather than in their essence." As a translator, he was generally admitted to have no superior in the English tongue, his skill was unvarying and absolutely reliable. Even here it might be doubted whether he ever attained the wonderful success sometimes achieved in single instances, as, for instance, in Mrs. Sarah Austen's "Many a Year is in its Grave," which, under the guise of a perfect translation, yet gives a higher and finer touch than that of the original poem of R 點 kert. But taking Longfellow's great gift in this direction as it was, we can see that it was somewhat akin to this quality of "composition," rather than of inspiration, which marked his poems.

He could find it delightful

"To lie And gaze into a summer sky And watch the trailing clouds go by Like ships upon the sea."

But it is a vast step from this to Browning's mountain picture

"Toward it tilting cloudlets prest Like Persian ships to Salamis."

In Browning everything is vigorous and individualized. We see the ships, we know the nationality, we recall the very battle, and over these we see in imagination the very shape and movements of the clouds; but there is no conceivable reason why Longfellow's lines should not have been written by a blind man who knew clouds merely by the descriptions of others. The limitation of Longfellow's poems reveals his temperament. He was in his perceptions essentially of poetic mind, but always in touch with the common mind; as individual lives grow deeper, students are apt to leave Longfellow for Tennyson, just as they forsake Tennyson for Browning. As to action, the tonic of life, so far as he had it, was supplied to him through friends,--Sumner in America; Freiligrath in Europe,--and yet it must be remembered that he would not, but for a corresponding quality in his own nature, have had just such friends as these. He was not led by his own convictions to leave his study like Emerson and take direct part as a contestant in the struggles of the time. It is a curious fact that Lowell should have censured Thoreau for not doing in this respect just the thing which Thoreau ultimately did and Longfellow did not. It was, however, essentially a difference of temperament, and it must be remembered that Longfellow wrote in his diary under date of December 2, 1859, "This will be a great day in our history; the date of a new Revolution,-- quite as much needed as the old one. Even now as I write, they are leading old John Brown to execution in Virginia, for attempting to rescue slaves! This is sowing the wind to reap the whirlwind, which will come soon."

His relations with Whittier remained always kindly and unbroken. They dined together at the Atlantic Club and Saturday Club, and Longfellow wrote of him in 1857, "He grows milder and mellower, as does his poetry." He went to Concord sometimes to dine with Emerson, "and meet his philosophers, Alcott, Thoreau, and Channing." Or Emerson came to Cambridge, "to take tea," giving a lecture at the Lyceum, of which Longfellow says, "The lecture good, but not of his richest and rarest. His subject 'Eloquence.' By turns he was grave and jocose, and had some striking views and passages. He lets in a thousand new lights, side-lights, and cross-lights, into every subject." When Emerson's collected poems are sent him, Longfellow has the book read to him all the evening and until late at night, and writes of it in his diary: "Throughout the volume, through the golden mist and sublimation of fancy, gleam bright veins of purest poetry, like rivers running through meadows. Truly, a rare volume; with many exquisite poems in it, among which I should single out 'Monadnoc,' 'Threnody,' 'The Humble-Bee,' as containing much of the quintessence of poetry." Emerson's was one of the five portraits drawn in crayon by Eastman Johnson, and always kept hanging in the library at Craigie House; the others being those of Hawthorne, Sumner, Felton, and Longfellow himself. No one can deny to our poet the merits of absolute freedom from all jealousy and of an invariable readiness to appreciate those classified by many critics as greater than himself. He was one of the first students of Browning in America, when the latter was known chiefly by his "Bells and Pomegranates," and instinctively selected the "Blot in the 'Scutcheon" as "a play of great power and beauty," as the critics would say, and as every one must say who reads it. He is an extraordinary genius, Browning, with dramatic power of the first order. "Paracelsus" he describes, with some justice, as "very lofty, but very diffuse." Of Browning's "Christmas Eve" he later writes, "A wonderful man is Browning, but too obscure," and later makes a similar remark on "The Ring and the Book." Of Tennyson he writes, as to "The Princess," calling it "a gentle satire, in the easiest and most flowing blank verse, with two delicious unrhymed songs, and many exquisite passages. I went to bed after it, with delightful music ringing in my ears; yet half disappointed in the poem, though not knowing why. There is a discordant note somewhere."

One very uncertain test of a man of genius is his "table-talk." Surrounded by a group of men who were such masters of this gift as Lowell, Holmes, and T. G. Appleton, Longfellow might well be excused from developing it to the highest extent, and he also "being rather a silent man," as he says of himself, escaped thereby the tendency to monologue, which was sometimes a subject of complaint in regard to the other three. Longfellow's reticence and self-control saved him from all such perils; but it must be admitted, on the other hand, that when his brother collects a dozen pages of his "table-talk" at the end of his memoirs, or when one reads his own list of them in "Kavanagh," the reader feels a slight inadequacy, as of things good enough to be said, but not quite worth the printing. Yet at their best, they are sometimes pungent and telling, as where he says, "When looking for anything lost, begin by looking where you think it is not;" or, "Silence is a great peace-maker;" or, "In youth all doors open outward; in old age they all open inward," or, more thoughtfully, "Amusements are like specie payments. We do not much care for them, if we know we can have them; but we like to know they may be had," or more profoundly still, "How often it happens that after we know a man personally, we cease to read his writings. Is it that we exhaust him by a look? Is it that his personality gives us all of him we desire?" There are also included among these passages some thoroughly poetic touches, as where he says, "The spring came suddenly, bursting upon the world as a child bursts into a room, with a laugh and a shout, and hands full of flowers." Or this, "How sudden and sweet are the visitations of our happiest thoughts; what delightful surprises! In the midst of life's most trivial occupations,--as when we are reading a newspaper, or lighting a bed-candle, or waiting for our horses to drive round,--the lovely face appears, and thoughts more precious than gold are whispered in our ear."

The test of popularity in a poet is nowhere more visible than in the demand for autographs. Longfellow writes in his own diary that on November 25, 1856, he has more than sixty such requests lying on his table; and again on January 9, "Yesterday I wrote, sealed, and directed seventy autographs. To-day I added five or six more and mailed them." It does not appear whether the later seventy applications included the earlier sixty, but it is, in view of the weakness of human nature, very probable. This number must have gone on increasing. I remember that in 1875 I saw in his study a pile which must have numbered more than seventy, and which had come in a single day from a single high school in a Western city, to congratulate him on his birthday, and each hinting at an autograph, which I think he was about to supply.

At the time of his seventy-fourth birthday, 1881, a lady in Ohio sent him a hundred blank cards, with the request that he would write his name on each, that she might distribute them among her guests at a party she was to give on that day. The same day was celebrated by some forty different schools in the Western States, all writing him letters and requesting answers. He sent to each school, his brother tells us, some stanza with signature and good wishes. He was patient even with the gentleman who wrote to him to request that he would send his autograph in his "own handwriting." As a matter of fact, he had to leave many letters unanswered, even by a secretary, in his latest years.

It is a most tantalizing thing to know, through the revelations of Mr. William Winter, that Longfellow left certain poems unpublished. Mr. Winter says: "He said also that he sometimes wrote poems that were for himself alone, that he should not care ever to publish, because they were too delicate for publication."{105} Quite akin to this was another remark made by him to the same friend, that "the desire of the young poet is not for applause, but for recognition." The two remarks limit one another; the desire for recognition only begins when the longing for mere expression is satisfied. Thoroughly practical and methodical and industrious, Longfellow yet needed some self-expression first of all. It is impossible to imagine him as writing puffs of himself, like Poe, or volunteering reports of receptions given to him, like Whitman. He said to Mr. Winter, again and again, "What you desire will come, if you will but wait for it." The question is not whether this is the only form of the poetic temperament, but it was clearly his form of it. Thoreau well says that there is no definition of poetry which the poet will not instantly set aside by defying all its limitations, and it is the same with the poetic temperament itself.

{100 Scudder's Men and Letters, p. 68.}

{101 Life, ii. 19, 20.}

{102 The New England Poets, p. 141.}

{103 Life, ii. 189.}

{104 Tennyson's Life, by his son, i. 507.}

{105 Life, iii. 356.}

CHAPTER XXIV

LONGFELLOW AS A MAN

Longfellow always amused himself, as do most public men, with the confused and contradictory descriptions of his personal appearance: with the Newport bookseller who exclaimed, "Why, you look more like a sea captain than a poet!" and a printer who described him as "a hale, portly, fine-looking man, nearly six feet in height, well proportioned, with a tendency to fatness; brown hair and blue eyes, and bearing the general appearance of a comfortable hotel-keeper." More graphic still, and on the whole nearer to the facts, is this description by an English military visitor who met him at a reception in Boston in 1850. I happened upon the volume containing it amid a pile of literary lumber in one of the great antiquarian bookstores of London:--

"He was rather under the middle size, but gracefully formed, and extremely prepossessing in his general appearance. His hair was light-colored, and tastefully disposed. Below a fine forehead gleamed two of the most beautiful eyes I had ever beheld in any human head. One seemed to gaze far into their azure depths. A very sweet smile, not at all of the pensively-poetical character, lurked about the well-shaped mouth, and altogether the expression of Henry Wordsworth [sic] Longfellow's face was most winning. He was dressed very fashionably--almost too much so; a blue frock coat of Parisian cut, a handsome waistcoat, faultless pantaloons, and primrose-colored 'kids' set off his compact figure, which was not a moment still; for like a butterfly glancing from flower to flower, he was tripping from one lady to another, admired and courted by all. He shook me cordially by the hand, introduced me to his lady, invited me to his house, and then he was off again like a humming bird."{106}

A later picture by another English observer is contained in Lord Ronald Gower's "My Reminiscences." After a description of a visit to Craigie House, in 1878, he says: "If asked to describe Longfellow's appearance, I should compare him to the ideal representations of early Christian saints and prophets. There is a kind of halo of goodness about him, a benignity in his expression which one associates with St. John at Patmos saying to his followers and brethren, 'Little children, love one another!'... Longfellow has had the rare fortune of being thoroughly appreciated in his own country and in other countries during his lifetime; how different, probably, would have been the career of Byron, of Keats, or of Shelley, had it been thus with them! It would be presumptuous for me, and out of place, to do more here than allude to the universal popularity of Longfellow's works wherever English is spoken; I believe it is not an exaggeration to say that his works are more popular than those of any other living poet. What child is there who has not heard of 'Excelsior,' or of 'Evangeline,' of 'Miles Standish,' or of 'Hiawatha'? What songs more popular than 'The Bridge,' and 'I know a maiden fair to see'? Or who, after reading the 'Psalm of Life,' or the 'Footsteps of Angels,' does not feel a little less worldly, a little less of the earth, earthy? The world, indeed, owes a deep debt of gratitude to Henry Wadsworth Longfellow.... Bidding me note the beauty of the autumnal tints that make America in the 'fall' look as if rainbows were streaming out of the earth, Longfellow presented me with a goodly sample of the red and golden leaves of the previous autumn, which, although dry and faded, still glowed like gems; these leaves I brought away with me, and they now form a garland round the poet's portrait; a precious souvenir of that morning passed at Craigie House."{107}

Lord Ronald Gower then quotes the words used long since in regard to Longfellow by Cardinal Wiseman,--words which find an appropriate place here.

"'Our hemisphere,' said the Cardinal, 'cannot claim the honor of having brought him forth, but he still belongs to us, for his works have become as household words wherever the English language is spoken. And whether we are charmed by his imagery, or soothed by his melodious versification, or elevated by the moral teachings of his pure muse, or follow with sympathetic hearts the wanderings of Evangeline, I am sure that all who hear my voice will join with me in the tribute I desire to pay to the genius of Longfellow.'"{108}

"We have but one life here on earth," wrote Longfellow in his diary; "we must make that beautiful. And to do this, health and elasticity of mind are needful, and whatever endangers or impedes these must be avoided." It is not often that a man's scheme of life is so well fulfilled, or when fulfilled is so well reflected in his face and bearing, tinged always by the actual mark of the terrible ordeal through which he had passed. When Sydney Dobell was asked to describe Tennyson, he replied, "If he were pointed out to you as the man who had written the Iliad, you would answer, 'I can well believe it.'" This never seemed to be quite true of Tennyson, whose dark oriental look would rather have suggested the authorship of the Arab legend of "Antar" or of the quatrains of Omar Khayy. But it was eminently true of the picturesqueness of Longfellow in his later years, with that look of immovable serenity and of a benignity which had learned to condone all human sins. In this respect Turgenieff alone approached him, in real life, among the literary men I have known, and there is a photograph of the Russian which is often mistaken for that of the American.

Indeed, the beauty of his home life remained always visible. Living constantly in the same old house with its storied associations, surrounded by children and their friends, mingling with what remained of his earlier friends,--with his younger brother, a most accomplished and lovable person, forming one of his own family, and his younger sister living near him in a house of her own,--he was also easily the first citizen of the little University City. Giving readily his time and means to all public interests, even those called political, his position was curiously unlike that of the more wayward or detached poets. Later his two married daughters built houses close by and bore children, and the fields were full of their playmates, representing the exuberant life of a new generation. He still kept his health, and as he walked to and fro his very presence was a benediction. Some of his old friends had been unfortunate in life and were only too willing to seek his door; and even his literary enterprises, as for instance the "Poems of Places," were mainly undertaken for their sakes, that they might have employment and support.

It is a curious but indisputable fact that no house in Cambridge, even in the tenfold larger university circle of to-day, presents such a constant course of hospitable and refined social intercourse as existed at Craigie House in the days of Longfellow. Whether it is that professors are harder worked and more poorly paid, or only that there happens to be no one so sought after by strangers and so able, through favoring fortune, to receive them, is not clear. But the result is the same. He had troops of friends; they loved to come to him and he to have them come, and the comforts of creature refreshment were never wanting, though perhaps in simpler guise than now. It needs but to turn the pages of his memoirs as written by his brother to see that with the agreeable moderation of French or Italian gentlemen, he joined their daintiness of palate and their appreciation of choice vintages, and this at a time when the physiological standard was less advanced than now, and a judicious attention to the subject was for that reason better appreciated. His friends from Boston and Brookline came so constantly and so easily as to suggest a far greater facility of conveyance than that of to-day, although the real facts were quite otherwise. One can hardly wonder that the bard's muse became a little festive under circumstances so very favorable. His earlier circle of friends known as "the five of clubs" included Professor Felton, whom Dickens called "the heartiest of Greek professors;" Charles Sumner; George S. Hillard, Sumner's law partner; and Henry R. Cleveland, a retired teacher and educational writer. Of these, Felton was a man of varied learning, as was Sumner, an influence which made Felton jocose but sometimes dogged, and Sumner eloquent, but occasionally tumid in style. Hillard was one of those thoroughly accomplished men who fail of fame only for want of concentration, and Cleveland was the first to advance ideas of school training, now so well established that men forget their ever needing an advocate. He died young, and Dr. Samuel G. Howe, a man of worldwide fame as a philanthropist and trainer of the blind, was put in to fill the vacancy. All these five men, being of literary pursuits, could scarcely fail of occasionally praising one another, and were popularly known as "the mutual admiration society;" indeed, there was a tradition that some one had written above a review of Longfellow's "Evangeline" by Felton, to be found at the Athenem Library, the condensed indorsement, "Insured at the Mutual." At a later period this club gave place, as clubs will, to other organizations, such as the short-lived Atlantic Club and the Saturday Club; and at their entertainments Longfellow was usually present, as were also, in the course of time, Emerson, Holmes, Lowell, Agassiz, Whittier, and many visitors from near and far. Hawthorne was rarely seen on such occasions, and Thoreau never. On the other hand, the club never included the more radical reformers, as Garrison, Phillips, Bronson Alcott, Edmund Quincy, or Theodore Parker, and so did not call out what Emerson christened "the soul of the soldiery of dissent."

It would be a mistake to assume that on these occasions Longfellow was a recipient only. Of course Holmes and Lowell, the most naturally talkative of the party, would usually have the lion's share of the conversation; but Longfellow, with all his gentle modesty, had a quiet wit of his own and was never wholly a silent partner. His saying of Ruskin, for instance, that he had "grand passages of rhetoric, Iliads in nutshells;" of some one else, that "Criticism is double edged. It criticises him who receives and him who gives;"

his description of the contented Dutch tradesman "whose golden face, like the round and ruddy physiognomy of the sun on the sign of a village tavern, seems to say 'Good entertainment here;'" of Venice, that "it is so visionary and fairylike that one is almost afraid to set foot on the ground, lest he should sink the city;" of authorship, that "it is a mystery to many people that an author should reveal to the public secrets that he shrinks from telling to his most intimate friends;" that "nothing is more dangerous to an author than sudden success, because the patience of genius is one of its most precious attributes;" that "he who carries his bricks to the building of every one's house will never build one for himself;"--these were all fresh, racy, and truthful, and would bear recalling when many a brilliant stroke of wit had sparkled on the surface and gone under. As a mere critic he grew more amiable and tolerant as he grew older, as is the wont of literary men; and John Dwight, then the recognized head of the musical brotherhood of Boston, always maintained that Longfellow was its worst enemy by giving his warm indorsement to the latest comer, whatever his disqualifications as to style or skill.

Holmes said of him in a letter to Motley in 1873:--

"I find a singular charm in the society of Longfellow,--a soft voice, a sweet and cheerful temper, a receptive rather than aggressive intelligence, the agreeable flavor of scholarship without any pedantic ways, and a perceptible soupcon of the humor, not enough to startle or surprise or keep you under the strain of over-stimulation, which I am apt to feel with very witty people."

And ten years later, writing to a friend and referring to his verses on the death of Longfellow, printed in the "Atlantic Monthly," he said: "But it is all too little, for his life was so exceptionally sweet and musical that any voice of praise sounds almost like a discord after it."

Professor Rolfe has suggested that he unconsciously describes himself in "The Golden Legend," where Walter the Minnesinger says of Prince Henry:--

"His gracious presence upon earth Was as a fire upon a hearth; As pleasant songs, at morning sung, The words that dropped from his sweet tongue Strengthened our hearts; or, heard at night, Made all our slumbers soft and light."

He also points out that this is the keynote of the dedication of "The Seaside and the Fireside," the volume published in 1849.

"As one who, walking in the twilight gloom, Hears round about him voices as it darkens, And seeing not the forms from which they come, Pauses from time to time, and turns and hearkens;

"So walking here in twilight, O my friends! I hear your voices, softened by the distance, And pause, and turn to listen, as each sends His words of friendship, comfort, and assistance.

"Thanks for the sympathies that ye have shown! Thanks for each kindly word, each silent token, That teaches me, when seeming most alone, Friends are around us, though no word be spoken."

In another age or country Longfellow would have been laurelled, medalled, or ennobled; but he has had what his essentially republican spirit doubtless preferred, the simple homage of a nation's heart. He had his share of foreign honors; and these did not come from Oxford and Cambridge only, since in 1873 he was chosen a member of the Russian Academy of Sciences, and in 1877 of the Spanish Academy. At home he was the honored member of every literary club or association to which he cared to belong. In the half-rural city where he spent his maturer life--that which he himself described in "Hyperion" as "this leafy blossoming, and beautiful Cambridge"--he held a position of as unquestioned honor and reverence as that of Goethe at Weimar or Jean Paul at Baireuth. This was the more remarkable, as he rarely attended public meetings, seldom volunteered counsel or action, and was not seen very much in public. But his weight was always thrown on the right side; he took an unfeigned interest in public matters, always faithful to the traditions of his friend Sumner; and his purse was always easily opened for all good works. On one occasion there was something like a collision of opinion between him and the city government, when it was thought necessary for the widening of Brattle Street to remove the "spreading chestnut-tree" that once stood before the smithy of the village blacksmith, Dexter Pratt. The poet earnestly expostulated; the tree fell, nevertheless; but by one of those happy thoughts which sometimes break the monotony of municipal annals, it was proposed to the city fathers that the children of the public schools should be invited to build out of its wood, by their small subscriptions, a great armchair for the poet's study. The unexpected gift, from such a source, salved the offence, but it brought with it a penalty to Mr. Longfellow's household, for the kindly bard gave orders that no child who wished to see the chair should be excluded; and the tramp of dirty little feet through the hall was for many months the despair of housemaids. Thenceforward his name was to these children a household word; and the most charming feature of the festival held on the two hundred and fiftieth anniversary of the settlement of Cambridge (December 28, 1880) was the reception given by a thousand grammar-school children to the gray and courteous old poet, who made then and there, almost for the only time in his life, and contrary to all previous expectations, a brief speech in reply.

On that occasion he thus spoke briefly, at the call of the mayor, who presided, and who afterwards caused to be read by Mr. George Riddle, the verses "From My Arm-Chair," which the poet had written for the children. He spoke as follows:--

MY DEAR YOUNG FRIENDS,--I do not rise to make an address to you, but to excuse myself from making one. I know the proverb says that he who excuses himself accuses himself,--and I am willing on this occasion to accuse myself, for I feel very much as I suppose some of you do when you are suddenly called upon in your class room, and are obliged to say that you are not prepared. I am glad to see your faces and to hear your voices. I am glad to have this opportunity of thanking you in prose, as I have already done in verse, for the beautiful present you made me some two years ago. Perhaps some of you have forgotten it, but I have not; and I am afraid,--yes, I am afraid that fifty years hence, when you celebrate the three hundredth anniversary of this occasion, this day and all that belongs to it will have passed from your memory; for an English philosopher has said that the ideas as well as children of our youth often die before us, and our minds represent to us those tombs to which we are approaching, where, though the brass and marble remain, yet the inscriptions are effaced by time, and the imagery moulders away.

Again, upon his seventy-fifth birthday, there were great rejoicings in the Cambridge schools, as indeed in those of many other cities far and wide.

Craigie House, his residence, has already been described. In this stately old edifice dwelt the venerable poet, who was usually to be found in his ample study, rich with the accumulations of literary luxury. One might find him seated with Coleridge's inkstand before him, perhaps answering one of the vast accumulations of letters from the school children of Western cities--an enormous mass of correspondence, which was a little while a delight, and then became a burden. Before him was a carved bookcase containing a priceless literary treasure,--the various editions of his works, and, which was far more valuable, the successive manuscripts of each, carefully preserved and bound under his direction, and often extending to three separate copies: the original manuscript, the manuscript as revised for the printer, and the corrected proofs. More than once his friends urged him to build a fireproof building for these unique memorials, as Washington did for his own papers elsewhere; but the calm and equable author used to reply, "If the house burns, let its contents go also."

The wonder of Mr. Longfellow's later years was not so much that he kept up his incessant literary activity as that he did it in the midst of the constant interruptions involved in great personal popularity and fame. He had received beneath his roof every notable person who had visited Boston for half a century; he had met them all with the same affability, and had consented, with equal graciousness, to be instructed by Emerson and Sumner, or to be kindly patronized--as the story goes--by Oscar Wilde. From that room had gone forth innumerable kind acts and good deeds, and never a word of harshness. He retained to the last his sympathy with young people, and with all liberal and progressive measures. Indeed, almost his latest act of public duty was to sign a petition to the Massachusetts legislature for the relief of the disabilities still placed in that State upon the testimony of atheists.

Mr. Longfellow's general health remained tolerably good, in spite of advancing years, until within about three months of his death. After retiring to bed in apparent health one night, he found himself in the morning so dizzy as to be unable to rise, and with a pain in the top of his head. For a week he was unable to walk across the room on account of dizziness, and although it gradually diminished, yet neither this nor the pain in the head ever entirely disappeared, and there was great loss of strength and appetite. He accepted the situation at once, retreated to the security of his own room, refused all visitors outside of the family, and had a printed form provided for the acknowledgment of letters, leaving his daughters to answer them. During the last three months of his life he probably did not write three dozen letters, and though he saw some visitors, he refused many more. He might sometimes be seen walking on his piazza, or even in the street before the house, but he accepted no invitations, and confined himself mainly within doors. His seventy-fifth birthday, February 27, was passed very quietly at home, in spite of the many celebrations held elsewhere. On Sunday, March 19, he had a sudden attack of illness, not visibly connected with his previous symptoms. It was evident that the end was near, and he finally died of peritonitis on Friday afternoon, March 24, 1882.

It will perhaps be found, as time goes on, that the greatest service rendered by Longfellow--beyond all personal awakening or stimulus exerted on his readers--was that of being the first conspicuous representative, in an eminently practical and hard-working community, of the literary life. One of a circle of superior men, he was the only one who stood for that life purely and supremely, and thus vindicated its national importance. Among his predecessors, Irving had lived chiefly in Europe, and Bryant in a newspaper office. Among his immediate friends, Holmes stood for exact science, Lowell and Whittier for reform, Sumner for statesmanship, Emerson for spiritual and mystic values; even the shy Hawthorne for public functions at home and abroad. Here was a man whose single word, sent forth from his quiet study, reached more hearts in distant nations than any of these, and was speedily reproduced in the far-off languages of the world. Considered merely as an antidote to materialism, such a life was of incalculable value. Looking at him, the reign of the purely materialistic, however much aided by organizing genius, was plainly self-limited; the modest career of Longfellow outshone it in the world's arena. Should that reign henceforth grow never so potent, the best offset to its most arrogant claims will be found, for years to come, in the memory of his name.

{106 The Home Circle, London, October, 1850, iii. 249.}

{107 My Reminiscences, by Lord Ronald Gower, American edition, ii. 227, 228.}

{108 Ib., American edition, ii. 228.}

23474184R00088

Made in the USA
Middletown, DE
29 August 2015